The Birth of

AMERICAN FEMINISM

The Seneca Falls
Woman's Convention of 1848

The Birth of
AMERICAN FEMINISM

The Seneca Falls
Woman's Convention of 1848

Edited by

Virginia Bernhard
and
Elizabeth Fox-Genovese

BRANDYWINE PRESS • St. James, New York

ISBN: 1-881-089-34-7

1st Printing 1995

Telephone Orders: 1-800-345-1776

Printed in the United States of America

TABLE OF CONTENTS

PART 2
THE SENECA FALLS CONVENTION OF 1848

PART 3
THE FLOWERING OF THE WOMEN'S
MOVEMENT: *THE LILY* (1849–1856)

PART 4
THE MOMENTUM:
WOMEN'S RIGHTS CONVENTIONS
AFTER SENECA FALLS

PART 5
THE HISTORY AS PARTICIPANTS
REMEMBERED IT

EDITORS' NOTE

What happened at Seneca Falls, New York, in the summer of 1848 was a pivotal point in the history of women in the modern world. A meeting of men and women in a small Methodist chapel began the long and eventually rewarding struggle to win a measure of equality for women in the United States—a nation dedicated to the principle that "all men are created equal." Yet for much of this nation's history the Seneca Falls convention has been largely unheralded, and what went on during two fateful days in July has been little noticed. This collection of readings is designed to commemorate and memorialize that event with a selection of documents that illustrate women's awakenings to activism and reform in nineteenth-century America. Editorial notes have been kept to a minimum so that readers may draw their own conclusions about the ideology and goals of the women's movement.

The editors would like to thank Vivien E. Rose, the historian at the Women's Rights National Historical Park in Seneca Falls, New York, and Douglas Vigneron, archivist of the Seneca Falls Historical Society, for their invaluable assistance in this project. Others whose clerical skills and patience made this task easier were Mark Chance and Mary Rose Vento. Laura Crawley and Stacey Horstmann, with wonderful ingenuity, helped to identify and collect sources.

In some cases, paragraphing and punctuation have been altered for clarity.

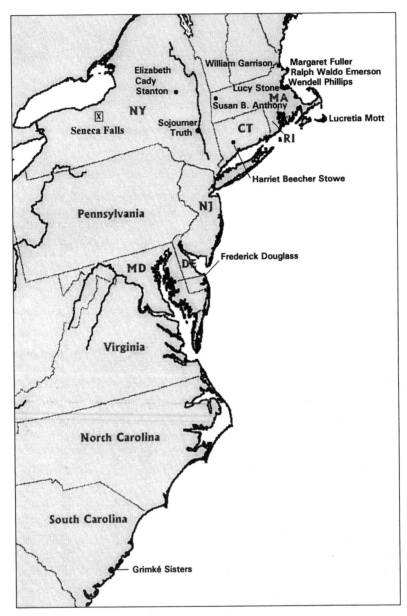

This map shows the birthplaces of some of the people who figured prominently in the movement that began at Seneca Falls in 1848.

INTRODUCTION

In 1776, when John Adams was attending the Contintental Congress in Philadelphia, his wife Abigail wrote to him from their farm at Braintree, Massachusetts, to "remember the ladies" when the time came to make laws for the new nation. "If particular care and attention are not paid to the ladies," she said, "we are determined to foment a rebellion, and will not hold ourselves bound to obey the laws in which we have no voice or representation." But more than fifty years after the founding of the republic, the women of the United States still had no voice. They were, as some of the first women's rights advocates eloquently expressed it, "civilly dead." The Declaration of Independence had promised equality for all, and the Constitution purported to be for "the people of the United States," yet for more than half of those people—all the white women and all the African American women and men who were slaves—the "Blessings of Liberty" were far from secure.

Women made up approximately half the population of the new nation, but they could not vote, or hold public office, or attend college, or study for any of the learned professions. Most African American women, like most African American men, were bound by an institution that denied them that most elemental of human rights, personal freedom. Native American women and men, though free, were not even entitled to citizenship. In white society, marriage promised a woman the pleasures of home and family but placed her under the complete domination of her husband. A married woman had little or no control over her property or income, and unless a prenuptial agreement existed, what was his was his, and what was hers was also his. Divorce in some states required an action by the legislature, and a failed marriage was usually thought to be the fault of the wife. (In almost every state, wife-beating "with a reasonable instrument" was legal as late as 1850.) If a divorcing couple had children, the husband almost always received custody.

As the new nation began, what one historian has called the "contagion of liberty" seemed to spread from state to state, transforming both law and society, but women's rights—or rather, the lack of them—remained unchanged. For middle- and upper-class white women, however, there was a new role: that of the "republican mother." While a woman could not have a voice in the making of laws in the young republic, she could at least have an influence by instilling "republican virtues" in her sons. But to do that properly she needed an education. As the political life of the new nation developed, so did a number of "female academies." In fact, the same year that saw the writing of the Constitution in Philadelphia saw the founding of the Young Ladies' Academy in that city. One of the Academy's trustees exulted that its students would be prepared to teach their sons "the principles of liberty and government." In Massachusetts Judith Sargent Murray in a 1790 essay, "On the Equality of the Sexes," wrote, "I expect to see our young women forming a new era in female history." But by the time of her death in 1820, Murray's expectations had not been realized.

Despite a flurry of interest in women's education in the late eighteenth century, the vast majority of women in the early republic, like their grandmothers and great-grandmothers in colonial America, did not receive much schooling. Reading and writing were rare accomplishments for a woman. In New England, for example, where there were more schools than in the middle and southern colonies at the end of the colonial period, fewer than half the women involved in the making of wills could sign their names. Literacy is difficult to measure, but it is safe to say that in 1800 a majority of women in the new nation could not write, and a significant number could not read. That is not quite so shocking as it seems, considering the nature of American society at a time when most families lived on farms or plantations, and nine out of ten people made their living from the soil. For ordinary folk, book learning was not essential, and for females, churning butter and weaving cloth were far more valuable skills than conjugating verbs or writing essays. For the majority of Americans of both sexes, schooling was difficult to come by until well into the nineteenth century.

The new country's population grew from nearly four million people in 1790 to over seventeen million by 1840, and in that fifty years—less than the space of two generations—technology, industry, and ideology wrought profound changes in American life. A textile mill in Lowell, Massachusetts, began to employ women workers. Towns and cities, nourished by a growing network of canals, rivers, and roads, bustled with new markets and new ideas. Religious revivals swept over the land, stirring rural communities, invigorating urban congregations. In the 1830s a wave of evangelical fervor known as the Second Great Awakening spread across New York, with so many hellfire sermons that part of the state was waggishly called the "burned-over district." Public schools increased in number, seminaries and academies flourished, and many new colleges were founded.

Numbers of better-educated, reform-minded men and women turned their attention to prisons and asylums, to the sorrows of brothels and saloons, and created new societies dedicated to social change: the American Society for the Promotion of Temperance (1826), the American Peace Society (1828), the American Anti-Slavery Society (1833), and the American Female Reform Society (1834) were only a few of the associations that emerged in an age of reform. This activism was not limited to the middle classes. In the 1830s working men in New York organized a political party, and in Massachusetts the young women workers in Lowell's textile mill formed the Lowell Female Labor Reform Association. The French writer, Alexis de Tocqueville, observed in *Democracy in America* (1835) that "Americans of all ages, all conditions, and all dispositions, constantly form associations. They have not only commercial and manufacturing companies, in which all take part, but associations of a thousand other kinds, religious, moral, serious, futile, general or restricted, enormous or diminutive."

While reforming drunkards and rescuing prostitutes were certainly admirable activities, the cause that generated the most moral fervor in the 1830s was the issue that would sunder the republic in another generation: slavery. As slavery spread westward in the first quarter of the nineteenth century, with the admission of Alabama, Mississippi, Louisiana, and Missouri to the Union, and as a Virginia slave named Nat Turner horrified the nation with a rebellion that killed over sixty whites in 1831, the "peculiar institution" fastened itself upon consciences North and South with very different results. The American Anti-Slavery Society, founded in 1833, soon had chapters scattered everywhere except in the South. In New England, New York, and the newer states of Ohio, Indiana, and Illinois, abolition societies multiplied; while in Virginia, the Carolinas, and the rest of the South, postmasters refused to handle anti-slavery literature and slave owners staunchly defended their right to own human property.

In a republic founded on the ideals of liberty and equality, it is no wonder that abolition drew the most dedicated individuals to its cause. Women as well as men could deplore the paradox of slavery in the land of freedom and could feel the moral outrage against the holding of human beings in bondage. But, ironically, in the age of reform, women reformers themselves were held in another kind of bondage, that imposed upon their sex by custom and convention, a set of gender prescriptions that, among other things, decreed that a woman's place was in the home, and that speaking in public before an audience of men would "unsex" her.

This view of women as delicate creatures, confined to private spaces and excluded from public discourse, developed as the nation's first industrial and urban growth began. As towns and cities grew, and commerce enlarged beyond the bounds of shop and local market, a quiet revolution transformed the lives of the nation's families: home and workplace, for hundreds of years under the same roof, began to separate. Woman's proper "sphere" was the home; man's, the public spaces of business and politics. The ideal woman was a creature of hearth and home: pious, virginal until marriage, skilled in all the domestic arts, and above all, submissive to her husband. The male author of a book entitled *The Sphere and Duties of Woman* wrote that marriage was "that sphere for which woman was originally intended, and to which she is so exactly fitted to adorn and bless, as the wife, the mistress of a home, the solace, the aid and the counselor of that ONE, for whose sake alone the world is of any consequence to her."

How could such a sequestered individual take part in public life? She might be, and in fact was encouraged to be, active in societies composed of other women and devoted to various charitable causes, but she was not to soil herself in the public arena, elbow to elbow, as it were, with men. In 1834, for example, the Philadelphia Female Anti-Slavery Society allowed women to speak out—but only to each other. Nevertheless, similar societies soon appeared in other cities. As time passed, some women, employing abolitionist rhetoric, became conscious of their own subordinate position in a society that confined them to "woman's sphere"—home and family—while giving to men the opportunities for public action. One such woman was Elizabeth Cady Stanton (1815–1902) who was to devote most of her long and productive life to the cause of women's rights.

Born in Johnstown, New York, a small industrial community overlooking the Mohawk River Valley, Elizabeth grew up surrounded by wealth, privilege, a houseful of servants, and the painful knowledge that her father wished she had been a boy. Of the eleven children born to the Cadys, only Elizabeth and three of her sisters lived past twenty. Judge Daniel Cady mourned the deaths of five sons, and nothing the young Elizabeth could do to please him made up for that. She studied Greek; she learned to ride; she read her father's law books; but the highest praise she could win from him was "Ah, you should have been a boy." She longed to go to college, but no college in that day admitted women, and so she was educated at the Troy Female Seminary. In 1840, against her parents' wishes, twenty-five-year-old Elizabeth married an abolitionist and journalist, Henry Stanton. She met him at the home of her cousin, Gerrit Smith, who was himself devoted to the antislavery cause. Elizabeth shared Henry Stanton's passion for reform (they agreed to omit the word "obey" from their marriage ceremony), and their honeymoon was a trip to London to attend the World Anti-Slavery Convention in 1840. A number of other American abolitionists, men and women, were also in attendance, and it was there that Elizabeth met the woman who would become her lifelong friend and collaborator in the cause of women's rights, Lucretia Coffin Mott (1793–1880).

A Nantucket sea captain's daughter, brought up as a devout Quaker, Lucretia Coffin saw women taking part as equals in the Society of Friends, and in a community where most of the men spent much of their time at sea, she also saw women managing households and businesses without a male presence. Educated in Boston, and then at a Quaker boarding school near Poughkeepsie, New York, she was made assistant teacher at that school at age fifteen. In 1811, eighteen-year-old Lucretia married a former fellow teacher, James Mott. Their marriage would last fifty-seven years.

Between 1812 and 1828 she bore him six children, four daughters and two sons, one of whom died in infancy. Religious concerns after her son's death deepened her faith, and in 1821 Lucretia Mott became a Quaker minister. Following Quaker teachings on the evil of slavery, she soon gave up using cotton cloth and cane sugar—the products of slave labor. In 1834 she helped found the Philadelphia Female Anti-Slavery Society, and in 1838 she was one of the organizers of the Anti-Slavery Convention of American Women. She calmly braved the wrath of anti-abolitionist mobs who set fire to a building in which she spoke, threatened her house, and tarred and feathered a fellow abolitionist. In that instance she demanded that the mob take her instead of her male colleague, declaring, "I ask no courtesy at your hands on account of my sex."

Lucretia Mott met Elizabeth Cady Stanton in London at the Anti-Slavery Convention in the summer of 1840, when Mott was forty-seven and Stanton twenty-five. When they, along with all the other women present, were denied seats on the convention floor and relegated to the gallery, the two shared their indignation at this demeaning treatment and agreed that something ought to be done about women's rights. Age was no barrier to their friendship. Both were intellectually gifted, strong-willed, energetic women, and both had experienced firsthand the discrimination against their sex. Arm in arm, they walked about London together, the one diminutive, intense-looking, with dark eyes and graying hair; the other a slender young woman whose cherubic face and ringlets belied her feminist convictions. They vowed to keep in touch, but the Motts lived in Philadelphia, and the Stantons, after two years in Johnstown and five years in Boston, settled in Seneca Falls, in upstate New York. After Boston—where the Stantons had numbered among their friends the ex-slave-turned-abolitionist Frederick Douglass, the poets John Greenleaf Whittier and James Russell Lowell, the novelist Nathaniel Hawthorne, and the Transcendentalists Theodore Parker, Bronson Alcott, and Ralph Waldo Emerson—young Mrs. Stanton found life in Seneca Falls very dull indeed. She found no one among its 4,000 people who shared her interests, and the incessant, repetitive demands of running a household weighed heavily upon her. She now had three small boys, born in 1842, 1844, and 1845. She wrote letters to friends and tried to find solace in religion, but longed for intellectual stimulation. Once she managed to spend a day in Boston with Lucretia Mott, and again the two talked of women's rights. They even considered holding a women's rights meeting in Boston. Stanton also discussed women's rights with Frederick Douglass, but nothing came of the plan for a convention. At the time, Lucretia Mott was deeply involved in Quaker religious controversies and was not in good health. She may have declined to take an active role, and Stanton may have felt unequal to acting alone. The two continued to correspond, but it was not until 1848, when the Motts paid a visit to Waterloo, New York, three miles from Seneca Falls, that the two women met again. On a July afternoon, these two and three of their friends decided to take a bold step: they resolved to hold a women's rights convention at

Seneca Falls. Inspired by young Elizabeth Cady Stanton's passionate talk of women's domestic drudgery and inferior status, they decided to act. The other women were Lucretia Mott's youngest sister, Martha Coffin Wright of Auburn, New York, and Jane Hunt and Mary Ann McClintock, both of Waterloo. They were not radical feminists; they were all respectable wives and mothers, who, as Stanton would later put it, had "souls large enough to feel the wrongs of others."

They wasted no time: that very day they persuaded the pastor of the Wesleyan Methodist Chapel in Seneca Falls to let them use his building for their meeting, and the next day, July 14, 1848, the *Seneca County Courier* carried a brief notice of a convention to discuss the "condition and rights of women" on July 19–20. On Sunday, July 16, the women met again at the home of Mary Ann McClintock to plan their meeting. It was Elizabeth Cady Stanton's enthusiasm and eloquence that had galvanized them to this historic act. Many years later the table around which they sat in the McClintock parlor would stand at the head of her casket at her funeral. (It is now at the Smithsonian Institution in Washington, D.C.) The group was new to women's rights, but they were not amateurs at reform. All but Elizabeth Cady Stanton were Quakers, familiar with the proceedings of assemblies and meetings, and all five women had had experience with the machinery of reform movements, with agendas and resolutions, speeches and petitions of protest. Casting about for a model, they decided to write a protest document based on the Declaration of Independence.

Elizabeth Cady Stanton drafted it, and the "Declaration of Sentiments," with "man" replacing George III as the usurper of rights, was ready for the convention on the following Tuesday. With its ringing condemnation of the "repeated injuries and usurpations on the part of man toward woman," the document sets forth a list of eighteen wrongs that would take women seventy-five years and more to put right: some, like the promise of equality in the Declaration of Independence, are still being realized. Lucretia Mott insisted that women's economic state, the inequities of property rights, wages, and educational opportunities, be addressed. Stanton argued that woman suffrage was the crucial key to women's advancement, and included in the women's grievances the denial of the right to vote. But, as the next several decades would prove, woman suffrage was a notion many women as well as most men considered either politically unwise or radical and threatening to the social order.

Seneca Falls, New York, was an unlikely place for a revolutionary convention. Located almost 200 miles west of Albany, it was an industrial town with some two dozen factories that produced, among other things, cotton cloth, paper, leather, water pumps, and window sashes. In 1848 it boasted six churches, four hotels, and one newspaper. But Seneca Falls was far from isolated. Another revolution of the early 1800s, sometimes called the "Transportation Revolution," connected Seneca Falls to the larger world: two canals, the Seneca and the Cayuga, linked the town to the Erie Canal, and thus by water, to the Hudson River and the Atlantic seaboard. Railroad tracks ran east to Syracuse, west to Rochester. Where railroads went, the telegraph, invented in 1844, soon followed, making communication with Boston, New York, and Philadelphia a matter of minutes, not days. Winters in upstate New York meant heavy snows, but summers, except for an occasional heat wave, were pleasantly mild.

The weather was warm on the morning of July 19. Although Lucretia Mott had cautioned that attendance at the meeting might be small "owing to the busy time with the farmers' harvests," the rutted roads to the Wesleyan Methodist Chapel were crowded with carts and carriages. When Stanton, Mott, and the other organizers arrived at the chapel, they found to their dismay that the building was locked. After a frantic and fruitless scramble to locate the minister with the key, Stanton had her young nephew hoisted through one of the windows to open the door. (The boy was the son of her sister, Harriet Cady Eaton, who had come to attend the convention.) When at last the meeting convened at 11:00 a.m., it was not Stanton, or Mott, or any of the other woman organizers who spoke first, but James Mott. Mindful of custom and propriety, the founders of American feminism dared not offend public sensibilities by having a female speak in public—even to a gathering of incipient feminists. And so it was Lucretia Mott's husband who presided over the first women's rights convention in American history. Thomas McClintock, husband of another of the organizers, also took a turn at presiding.

As Elizabeth Cady Stanton remembered this event years later, all the husbands were supportive, and some attended the meeting. Henry Stanton, however, was notably absent. He had helped to draft some of the resolutions, but like Lucretia Mott, opposed the resolution on woman suffrage, and feared that his wife would be involved in "a farce." Claiming he had pressing business elsewhere, he betook himself to Albany. Meanwhile, Judge Daniel Cady, Elizabeth's father, reportedly rushed to Seneca Falls fearing for his daughter's sanity. Her older sister Tryphena Bayard wept over Elizabeth's involvement in such a radical cause, but her younger sister, Harriet Eaton, attended the convention and signed its Declaration of Sentiments, though she later rescinded her signature at the urging of her husband.

The first day of the meeting drew a crowd of over a hundred, including about thirty men. After James Mott called the meeting to order, Elizabeth Cady Stanton read the Declaration of Sentiments, section by section, with comments and discussion by the audience. In the afternoon session, when a paper was circulated to record the signatures of those who approved of the Declaration, sixty-eight women and thirty-two men, including the abolitionist Frederick Douglass, put their names to it. The next morning at ten, the group reconvened, larger in size (by the final session, attendance numbered around 300) still under the guiding hand of James Mott, to hear the previous day's minutes read, and to listen to a final reading of the Declaration of Sentiments, which was then unanimously adopted. The rest of the time was devoted to the presentation and discussion of twelve resolutions.

These calls for action, which the *Seneca County Courier* described as "spirited and spicy," were debated one by one. The ninth, calling upon women to "secure to themselves their sacred right to the elective franchise," aroused a vigorous opposition. Many felt that such a radical proposal would make the women's meeting the object of ridicule, and would thus eclipse the other less controversial resolutions. Elizabeth Cady

Stanton made an impassioned plea for the suffrage resolution, arguing that "drunkards, idiots, horseracing rumselling rowdies, ignorant foreigners, and silly boys" could all exercise their right to the ballot box, while women were denied it. "The right is ours," she said. "Have it we must. Use it we will. The pens, the tongues, the fortunes, the indomitable wills of many women are already pledged to secure this right." Frederick Douglass also spoke eloquently in support of Stanton's claim, and the resolution passed. For the first time in the history of the republic, women had publicly demanded the right to vote.

That evening at 7:00 p.m. the final session took place, with Thomas McClintock as presiding officer. He read from Blackstone's *Commentaries* a section on women in English common law. Lucretia Mott introduced an additional resolution calling for the "zealous and untiring efforts of both men and women, for the overthrow of the monopoly of the pulpit, and for the securing to woman of equal participation with men in the various trades, professions, and commerce." The resolution passed. With closing speeches by Frederick Douglass, Mary Ann McClintock, and Lucretia Mott, the first women's rights convention ended. No strategy had been planned, no tactics devised, but the struggle to gain equality for women in American society had begun.

The organizers of the Seneca Falls convention had expected criticism, but perhaps even they were unprepared for the torrent of sarcasm and ridicule that rolled in upon them in the next few weeks. In New York and Philadelphia, newspapers extolled the virtues of traditional women and condemned the newly-declared advocates of women's rights as heretics, radicals, and old maids. The Seneca Falls convention and the Declaration of Sentiments were dismissed as the work of unnatural women, but they were discussed nonetheless, and Elizabeth Cady Stanton was pleased. "There is no danger of the Woman Question dying for want of notice," she wrote wryly.

In the aftermath of the Seneca Falls convention, there were other meetings in other places, the first one only two weeks later. In a church in Rochester, New York, women gathered in the name of women's rights. In Massachusetts there were meetings, in Pennsylvania there were meetings, and as far away as

Ohio and Indiana there were meetings. By 1850 there would be a national women's rights convention attended by over a thousand men and women. After that, there were annual conventions, and Elizabeth Cady Stanton and Lucretia Mott continued throughout their long lives to be involved in the cause of women's rights.

Back in Philadelphia, Mott was active in Quaker circles, in the temperance movement, and even in helping runaway slaves escape. After the Civil War, she worked to raise money for schools for newly freed slaves in the South. Active until her death in 1880 at the age of 87, she had devoted most of her life to causes of social reform.

Three years after the Seneca Falls convention, Elizabeth Cady Stanton met the woman whose name became almost a synonym for feminism, and with whom she would collaborate in that cause for the rest of her life. Susan Brownell Anthony (1820–1906) did not attend the 1848 women's rights convention, but her parents and her younger sister did. She and Stanton met in 1851, when Anthony visited Seneca Falls as the house guest of Amelia Bloomer (who popularized "bloomers" as a liberating costume for women in the 1850s). Susan B. Anthony, already involved in temperance and abolition, was soon won over to women's rights, and for the next fifty years she and Stanton were linked in that long and difficult struggle. The two women were a study in contrasts. Anthony, who never married, was plain in appearance, with straight hair, a slight squint in one eye, and a downturned mouth that gave her a dour expression. A Quaker, she favored simple dress over fashionable frills. But she had a keen mind and a talent for organization, and a zest for reform that matched Stanton's own. When the Civil War came, they organized the Women's Loyal National League to work for ending slavery by constitutional amendment.

With freedom for the nation's nearly four million slaves, however, came a dilemma for women's rights: If the newly freed slaves, now entitled to citizenship, could vote, why not women? Until 1868, when the Fourteenth Amendment introduced the word "male" into the Constitution, there had been nothing in that document that prohibited women voting. But the controversial Fourteenth Amendment, in guaranteeing the rights of citizenship to "all persons born or naturalized in the United States," now stipulated that "when the right to vote ... is denied to any of the male inhabitants" of a state [meaning slaves] the basis of representation in that state would be proportionately reduced. Stanton, Anthony, and other feminists were outraged. In 1869 they founded the National Woman Suffrage Organization, but the momentum of the women's rights movement suffered a serious setback in the last quarter of the nineteenth century. Race had won over gender in the national arena, and in the South, especially, race would keep woman suffrage out of public discourse until the twentieth century. Women voting might mean African American women voting, and that, in a region already embittered over the presence of African American male voters, was unthinkable to the majority of southerners of both genders. Even some of the freed slaves, hoping to curry favor with whites, espoused anti-woman suffrage views.

But Elizabeth Cady Stanton, Susan B. Anthony, and other feminists did not give up the struggle during these years. In 1876 they composed the Women's Declaration of Rights, which was read at the Centennial celebration in Philadelphia on July 4, 1876. In 1878 Elizabeth Cady Stanton, who had first brought the issue of woman suffrage into public discourse in 1848, persuaded a senator to place before Congress a federal woman suffrage amendment, almost identical in wording to the controversial Fifteenth Amendment ratified only eight years before:

> The right of citizens of the United States to vote shall not be denied or abridged by the United States or by any State on account of sex.
> [The Fifteenth Amendment reads, "on account of race, color, or previous condition of servitude."]
> Congress shall have the power to enforce this article by appropriate legislation.

Introduced again and again, to every succeeding Congress, this amendment would finally pass in 1920 as the Nineteenth Amendment. The battle for woman suffrage had taken seventy-two years to win, but the opening shots had been fired at Seneca Falls, New York, in 1848.

*   *   *

The Seneca Falls Convention of 1848 raises a number of important questions: Why did the movement emerge in the 1840s, and not before? Why did the struggle for woman suffrage last until 1920? How "radical" were the demands and the actions of the 1840s feminists? Did they seek equality with men, or did they look to the establishment of a new role for women? Did they seek to address the needs of all women, or just those of white, middle-class women? These are questions that more recent feminism has also had to confront.

The evidence presented here suggests other questions: How was nineteenth-century feminism related to other reforms, such as abolitionism? To what extent were the first feminists influenced by their upbringing, their education, and public opinion? What roles did men play in the nineteenth-century struggle for women's rights?

Above all, Seneca Falls opened a new discussion about the meaning of freedom in the United States. Today, the demand that women enjoy and participate equally in the benefits of civic freedom seems so natural as to be modest. Yet in its time and place, it was radical. In 1848, the women of no country in the world enjoyed the right to vote, which many countries still denied to men. Most people regarded it as "natural" that men, as heads of households, should represent their wives in the public sphere and be responsible for them in the private sphere. This responsibility was widely taken to include the right to control their property and even to enforce discipline upon them. To be sure, Christianity recognized the equality of women and men, but only in the sense of the equality of souls before God. And only occasional groups of radicals had previously attempted to implement Christian ideals of freedom and equality in the world. In challenging traditional norms about women's place in the family, society, and the polity, the women of Seneca Falls were implicitly—and often explicitly—calling into question the fundamental principles of social life.

In general, the women of Seneca Falls muted the extent of their radicalism, suggesting that the implementation of personal and civic freedom for women would merely implement basic justice without otherwise transforming the structure of society. But some, notably Elizabeth Cady Stanton, assuredly understood that that implementation would transform society and the meaning of freedom itself. It is surely a measure of the revolutionary significance of their "modest" project that American society is still trying to understand and come to terms with its implications.

PART 1

WOMEN AS ACTIVISTS: THE BEGINNINGS

The Clergy's Opposition

A Pastoral Letter from Massachusetts, 1837

The cause of women's rights drew far more criticism than support in the nineteenth century. In the years before the Civil War, women who dared to speak in public about any reform issue—abolitionism, temperance, or women's rights—were viewed as unfeminine and were often harshly criticized. In the 1830s, when slavery began to gnaw at the nation's conscience, many women felt the need to make their voices heard. The criticism they endured for enlisting in the antislavery cause awakened some of them to the fact of their own inequality: thus abolitionism and feminism were linked. The following document is an excerpt from a pastoral letter of the General Association of Congregational Churches in Massachusetts, designed to be read in churches across the state.

...The appropriate duties and influence of woman are clearly stated in the New Testament. Those duties and that influence are unobtrusive and private, but the source of mighty power. When the mild, dependent, softening influence of woman upon the sternness of man's opinions is fully exercised, society feels the effects of it in a thousand forms. The power of woman is in her dependence, flowing from the consciousness of that weakness which God has given her for her protection, and

Source: Letter of "the General Association of Massachusetts Congregational (Orthodox) to the Churches under their care" (1837), Elizabeth Cady Stanton, Susan B. Anthony et al., *The History of Woman Suffrage* (6 vols.; New York, 1881–1922; reprint, New York, 1969), vol. 1.

19

which keeps her in those departments of life that form the character of individuals and of the nation. There are social influences which females use in promoting piety and the great objects of Christian benevolence which we cannot too highly commend. We appreciate the unostentatious prayers and efforts of woman in advancing the cause of religion at home and abroad; in Sabbath-schools; in leading religious inquirers to the pastors for instruction; and in all such associated effort as becomes the modesty of her sex; and earnestly hope that she may abound more and more in these labors of piety and love.

But when she assumes the place and tone of man as a public reformer, our care and protection of her seem unnecessary; we put ourselves in self-defence against her; she yields the power which God has given her for protection, and her character becomes unnatural. If the vine, whose strength and beauty is to lean upon the trellis-work and half conceal its clusters, thinks to assume the independence and the overshadowing nature of the elm, it will not only cease to bear fruit, but fall in shame and dishonor into the dust. We cannot, therefore, but regret the mistaken conduct of those who encourage females to bear an obtrusive and ostentatious part in measure of reform, and countenance any of that sex who so far forget themselves as to itinerate in the character of public lecturers and teachers.—We especially deplore the intimate acquaintance and promiscuous conversation of females with regard to things "which ought not to be named"; by which that modesty and delicacy which is the charm of domestic life, and which constitutes the true influence of woman in society, is consumed, and the way opened, as we apprehend, for degeneracy and ruin. We say these things, not to discourage proper influences against sin, but to secure such reformation as we believe is Scriptural, and will be permanent.

The Grimké Sisters on Women's Rights

When Angelina and Sarah Grimké, daughters of a Charleston, South Carolina, slaveholder, left the land of their birth and dedicated themselves to the cause of antislavery, they scandalized southerners and captivated northern abolitionists. Angelina (1805–1879), the younger of the two, wrote An Appeal to the Christian Women of the South *in 1836, in a futile attempt to enlist southern women in the antislavery movement. The American Anti-Slavery Society applauded her efforts and those of her sister, Sarah (1792–1873), who wrote* An Epistle to the Clergy of the Southern States *in 1836. As Quakers, first in Philadelphia and then in New York, the Grimkés became active lecturers and writers in the abolitionist movement, and both took up the cause of women's rights. Sarah published* Letters on the Equality of the Sexes and the Condition of Women *in 1838, ten years before the Seneca Falls Convention. The following selection is an extract from one such letter.*

LETTER OF SARAH GRIMKÉ TO THE BOSTON FEMALE ANTI-SLAVERY SOCIETY, 1837

Brookline, 1837

During the early part of my life, my lot was cast among the butterflies of the *fashionable* world; and of this class of women, I

Source: Sarah Grimké, *Letters on the Equality of the Sexes and the Condition of Women* (Boston, 1838).

Sarah Moore Grimké.
*(Courtesy: New York Public
Library)*

am constrained to say, both from experience and observation,
that their education is miserably deficient; that they are taught
to regard marriage as the one thing needful, the only avenue to
distinction; hence to attract the notice and win the attention of
men, by their external charms is the chief business of fashionable girls.... Fashionable women regard themselves, and are
regarded by men as pretty toys or as mere instruments of pleasure; and the vacuity of mind, the heartlessness, the frivolity
which is the necessary result of this false and debasing estimate
of women, can only be fully understood by those who have min-
gled in the folly and wickedness of fashionable life....

There is another and much more numerous class in this
country, who are withdrawn by education or circumstances
from the circle of fashionable amusements, but who are brought
up with the dangerous and absurd idea, that *marriage* is a kind
of preferment; and that to be able to keep their husband's house,
and render his situation comfortable, is the end of her being.
Much that she does and says and thinks is done in reference to
this situation; and to be married is too often held up to the view
of girls as the *sine qua non* of human happiness and human existence. For this purpose more than for any other, I verily believe
the majority of girls are trained. This is demonstrated by the

imperfect education which is bestowed upon them, and the little pains taken to cultivate their minds, after they leave school, by the little time allowed them for reading, and by the idea being constantly inculcated, that although all household concerns should be attended to with scrupulous punctuality at particular seasons, the improvement of their intellectual capacities is only a secondary consideration, and may serve as an occupation to fill up the odds and ends of time. In most families, it is considered a matter of far more consequence to call a girl off from making a pie, or a pudding, than to interrupt her whilst engaged in her studies. This mode of training necessarily exalts, in their view, the animal above the intellectual and spiritual nature, and teaches women to regard themselves as a kind of machinery, necessary to keep the domestic engine in order, but of little value as the *intelligent* companions of men....

There is another class of women in this country, to whom I cannot refer, without feelings of the deepest shame and sorrow. I allude to our female slaves. Our southern cities are overwhelmed beneath a tide of pollution; the virtue of female slaves is wholly at the mercy of irresponsible tyrants, and women are bought and sold in our slave markets, to gratify the brutal lust of those who bear the name of Christians. In our slave States, if amid all her degradation and ignorance, a woman desires to preserve her virtue unsullied, she is either bribed or whipped into compliance, or if she dares resist her seducer, her life by the laws of some of the slave States may be, and has actually been sacrificed to the fury of disappointed passion. Where such laws do not exist, the power which is necessarily vested in the master over his property, leaves the defenceless slave entirely at his mercy and the sufferings of some females on this account, both physical and mental, are intense....

Nor does the colored woman suffer alone: the moral purity of the white woman is deeply contaminated. In the daily habit of seeing the virtue of her enslaved sister sacrificed without hesitancy or remorse, she looks upon the crimes of seduction and illicit intercourse without horror, and although not personally involved in the guilt, she loses that value for innocence in her own, as well as the other sex, which is one of the strongest safeguards to virtue.... In addition to all this, the female slaves suffer every species of degradation and cruelty, which the most wanton barbarity can inflict; they are indecently divested of their clothing, sometimes tied up and severely whipped, sometimes prostrated on the earth, while their naked bodies are torn by the scorpion lash.... Can any American woman look at these scenes of shocking licentiousness and cruelty, and fold her hands in apathy, and say, "I have nothing to do with slavery"? *She cannot, and be guiltless.*

* * *

Angelina Grimké, like her sister, linked the cause of antislavery with a call for women's activism. The following is an excerpt from one of her letters to Catharine Beecher, the sister of Harriet Beecher Stowe, in 1837. [Note: Lyman Beecher, referred to below, was Catharine and Harriet Beecher's father, the distinguished Congregationalist minister.]

LETTER FROM ANGELINA GRIMKÉ TO CATHARINE BEECHER, 1837

East Boylston, Mass. 10th mo. 2d, 1837

I have found the Anti-Slavery cause to be the high school of morals in our land—the school in which *human rights* are more fully investigated, and better understood and taught, than in any other. Here a great fundamental principle is uplifted and illuminated, and from this central light, rays innumerable stream all around. Human beings have *rights*, because they are *moral* beings: the rights of *all* men grow out of their moral nature; and as all men have the same moral nature, they have essentially the same rights. These rights may be wrested from the slave, but they cannot be alienated: his title to himself is as perfect *now*, as is that of Lyman Beecher: it is stamped on his moral being, and is, like it, imperishable. Now if rights are founded in

---

Source: Angelina E. Grimké, *Letters to Catharine E. Beecher, In Reply to an Essay on Slavery and Abolitionism, Addressed to A.E. Grimké* (Boston, 1838).

Angelina Emily Grimké.
*(Courtesy: New York Public
Library)*

the nature of our moral being, then the *mere circumstance of sex*
does not give to man higher rights and responsibilities, than to
woman. To suppose that it does, would be to deny the self-
evident truth, that the 'physical constitution is the mere instrument of the moral nature.' . . . My doctrine then is, that
whatever it is morally right for man to do, it is morally right for
woman to do. Our duties originate, not from difference of sex,
but from the diversity of our relations in life, the various gifts
and talents committed to our care, and the different eras in
which we live.

This regulation of duty by mere circumstance of sex, rather
than by the fundamental principle of moral being, has led to all
that multifarious train of evils flowing out of the anti-Christian
doctrine of masculine and feminine virtues. . . . Woman, instead
of being regarded as the equal of man, has uniformly been
looked down upon as his inferior, a mere gift to fill up the
measure of his happiness. . . . Let us examine the account of
her creation. 'And the rib which the Lord God had taken from
man, made he a woman, and brought her unto the man.' Not
as a gift—for Adam immediately recognized her *as a part of
himself*—('this is bone of my bone, and flesh of my flesh')—a
companion and equal, not one hair's breadth beneath him in the

majesty and glory of her moral being; not placed under his authority as a *subject*, but by his side, on the same platform of human rights, under the government of God only. This idea of woman's being 'the last best gift of God to man,' however pretty it may sound to the ears of those who love to discourse upon 'the poetry of romantic gallantry, and the generous promptings of chivalry,' has nevertheless been the means of sinking her from an *end* into a mere *means*—of turning her into an *appendage* to man, instead of recognizing her as a *part of man*—of destroying her individuality, and rights, and responsibilities, and merging her moral being in that of man. Instead of *Jehovah* being *her* king, *her* lawgiver, and *her* judge, she has been taken out of the exalted scale of existence in which He placed her, and subjected to the despotic control of man. . . .

I recognize no rights but *human* rights—I know nothing of men's rights and women's rights; for in Christ Jesus, there is neither male nor female. It is my solemn conviction, that, until this principle of equality is recognized and embodied in practice, the church can do nothing effectual for the permanent reformation of the world. . . . Now, I believe it is woman's right to have a voice in all the laws and regulations by which she is to be *governed*, whether in Church or State; and that the present arrangements of society, on these points are *a violation of human rights, a rank usurpation of power*, a violent seizure and confiscation of what is sacredly and inalienably hers—thus inflicting upon woman outrageous wrongs, working mischief incalculable in the social circle, and in its influence on the world producing only evil, and that continually. *If* Ecclesiastical and Civil governments are ordained of God, *then* I contend that woman has just as much right to sit in solemn council in Conventions, conferences, Associations and General Assemblies, as men—just as much right to it upon the throne of England, or in the Presidential chair of the United States. . . .

Woman in the Nineteenth Century (1845)

Margaret Fuller

The women who organized the Seneca Falls Convention in 1848 were not the first to point out that their sisters in the nineteenth century occupied an inferior status. At the close of the previous century, Mary Wollstonecraft's Vindication of the Rights of Women, *published in England in 1791, had sounded the first call to action. In the 1820s another Englishwoman, Frances Wright, came to the United States and shocked a citizenry unused to hearing a woman speak in public— especially a woman who argued for free love as well as women's equality. Catharine Beecher, the sister of Harriet Beecher Stowe, argued for what might be called domestic feminism—the power of women through their status as wives and mothers. Her* Treatise on Domestic Economy *was published in 1843. And in 1845 a young woman named Margaret Fuller, a friend of Ralph Waldo Emerson and one of the first woman journalists, wrote a book that remains a classic of feminist literature. Her* Woman in the Nineteenth Century *declared that women must develop both their individual natures and their public roles. Fuller took her own advice, traveling to Europe as a foreign correspondent, falling in love with an Italian revolutionary, bearing his child, and writing a treatise on the liberation of*

Source: Margaret Fuller, *Woman in the Nineteenth Century* (1845).

Italy. Had she been in the United States in 1848, she would no doubt have been part of the women's movement. But Margaret Fuller died at age forty when the ship on which she and her new family were returning sank off Fire Island, New York, in May 1850.

In the following excerpts from Woman in the Nineteenth Century, *Fuller points out the connection between the antislavery movement and the rights of women, argues for equality in marriage, and urges women to "rouse their latent powers."*

Of all its banners, none has been more steadily upheld, and under none have more valor and willingness for real sacrifices been shown, than that of the champions of the enslaved African. And this band it is which, partly from a natural following out of principles, partly because many women have been prominent in that cause, makes just now the warmest appeal in behalf of Woman.

Though there has been a growing liberality on this subject, yet society at large is not so prepared for the demands of this party, but that its members are and will be for some time coldly regarded as the Jacobins of their day.

"Is it not enough," cries the irritated trader, "that you have done all you could to break up the national union and thus destroy the prosperity of our country, but now you must be trying to break up family union, to take my wife away from the cradle and the kitchen-hearth to vote at polls and preach from a pulpit? Of course, if she does such things, she cannot attend to those of her own sphere. She is happy enough as she is. She has more leisure than I have—every means of improvement, every indulgence."

"Have you asked her whether she was satisfied with these *indulgences?*"

"No, but I know she is. She is too amiable to desire what would make me unhappy, and too judicious to wish to step beyond the sphere of her sex. I will never consent to have our peace disturbed by any such discussions."

" 'Consent—you?' It is not consent from you that is in question—it is assent from your wife."

"Am not I the head of my house?"

"You are not the head of your wife. God has given her a mind of her own."

"I am the head, and she the heart."

"God grant you play true to one another, then! I suppose I am to be grateful that you did not say she was only the hand. If the head represses no natural pulse of the heart, there can be no question as to your giving your consent. Both will be of one accord, and there needs but to present any question to get a full and true answer. There is no need of precaution, of indulgence, or consent. But our doubt is whether the heart *does* consent with the head, or only obeys its decrees with a passiveness that precludes the exercise of its natural powers, or a repugnance that turns sweet qualities to bitter, or a doubt that lays waste the fair occasions of life. It is to ascertain the truth that we propose some liberating measures."

Thus vaguely are these questions proposed and discussed at present. But their being proposed at all implies much thought and suggests more. Many women are considering within themselves what they need that they have not, and what they can have if they find they need it. Many men are considering whether women are capable of being and having more than they are and have, *and* whether, if so, it will be best to consent to improvement in their condition. . . .

The past year has seen action in the Rhode Island legislature to secure married women rights over their own property, where men showed that a very little examination of the subject could teach them much; an article in the *Democratic Review* on the same subject more largely considered, written by a woman impelled, it is said, by glaring wrong to a distinguished friend, having shown the defects in the existing laws and the state of opinion from which they spring; and an answer from the revered old man, J. Q. Adams. . . .

These symptoms of the times have come under my view quite accidentally: one who seeks may each month or week collect more.

The numerous party, whose opinions are already labeled and adjusted too much to their mind to admit of any new light, strive by lectures on some model woman of bridelike beauty and gentleness, by writing and lending little treatises intended to mark out with precision the limits of Woman's sphere and Woman's mission, to prevent other than the rightful shepherd from climbing the wall, or the flock from using any chance to go astray.

Without enrolling ourselves at once on either side, let us look upon the subject from the best point of view which today offers; no better, it is to be feared, than a high house-top. A high hilltop or at least a cathedral-spire would be desirable.

It may well be an Anti-Slavery party that pleads for Woman, if we consider merely that she does not hold property on equal terms with men; so that if a husband dies without making a will, the wife, instead of taking at once his place as head of the family, inherits only a part of his fortune, often brought him by herself, as if she were a child or ward only, not an equal partner.

We will not speak of the innumerable instances in which profligate and idle men live upon the earnings of industrious wives; or if the wives leave them and take with them the children to perform the double duty of mother and father, follow from place to place and threaten to rob them of the children, if deprived of the rights of a husband as they call them, planting themselves in their poor lodgings, frightening them into paying tribute by taking from them the children, running into debt at the expense of these otherwise so overtasked helots. Such instances count up by scores within my own memory. I have seen the husband who had stained himself by a long course of low vice, till his wife was wearied from her heroic forgiveness by finding that his treachery made it useless, and that if she would provide bread for herself and her children, she must be separate from his ill fame—I have known this man come to install himself in the chamber of a woman who loathed him, and say she should never take food without his company. I have known these men steal their children, whom they knew they had no means to maintain, take them into dissolute company, expose them to bodily danger, to frighten the poor woman to whom, it seems, the fact that she alone had borne the pangs of their birth and nourished their infancy does not give an equal right to them. I do believe that this mode of kidnaping—and it is frequent enough in all classes of society—will be by the next age viewed as it is by Heaven now, and that the man who avails himself of the shelter of men's laws to steal from a mother her own children, or arrogate any superior right in them, save that of superior virtue, will bear the stigma he deserves in common with him who steals grown men from their motherland, their hopes, and their homes.

I said we will not speak of this now; yet I *have* spoken, for the subject makes me feel too much. I could give instances that would startle the most vulgar and callous; but I will not, for the public opinion of their own sex is already against such men, and where cases of extreme tyranny are made known, there is private action in the wife's favor. But she ought not to need this, nor, I think, can she long. Men must soon see that as on their own ground Woman is the weaker party, she ought to have legal protection which would make such oppression impossible. But I would not deal with "atrocious instances" except in the way of illustration, neither demand from men a partial redress in some one matter, but go to the root of the whole. If principles could be established, particulars would adjust themselves aright. Ascertain the true destiny of Woman; give her legitimate hopes, and a standard within herself; marriage and all other relations would by degrees be harmonized with these.

But to return to the historical progress of this matter. Knowing that there exists in the minds of men a tone of feeling toward women as toward slaves, such as is expressed in the common phrase, "Tell that to women and children"; that the infinite soul can only work through them in already ascertained limits; that the gift of reason, Man's highest prerogative, is allotted to them in much lower degree; that they must be kept from mischief and melancholy by being constantly engaged in active labor, which is to be furnished and directed by those better able to think, &c., &c.—we need not multiply instances, for who can review the experience of last week without recalling words which imply, whether in jest or earnest, these views or views like these—knowing this, can we wonder that many reformers think that measures are not likely to be taken in behalf of women, unless their wishes could be publicly represented by women?

"That can never be necessary," cry the other side. "All men are privately influenced by women; each has his wife, sister, or female friends, and is too much biased by these relations to fail of representing their interests; and if this is not enough, let them propose and enforce their wishes with the pen. The beauty of home would be destroyed, the delicacy of the sex be violated, the dignity of halls of legislation degraded by an attempt to introduce them there. Such duties are inconsistent with those of a mother"; and then we have ludicrous pictures of ladies in hysterics at the polls, and senate chambers filled with cradles.

But if in reply we admit as truth that Woman seems destined by nature rather for the inner circle, we must add that the arrangements of civilized life have not been as yet such as to secure it to her. Her circle, if the duller, is not the quieter. If kept from "excitement," she is not from drudgery. Not only the Indian squaw carries the burdens of the camp, but the favorites of Louis XIV accompany him in his journeys, and the washerwoman stands at her tub and carries home her work at all seasons and in all states of health. Those who think the physical circumstances of Woman would make a part in the affairs of national government unsuitable are by no means those who think it impossible for Negresses to endure field work even during pregnancy, or for seamstresses to go through their killing labors.

As to the use of the pen, there was quite as much opposition to Woman's possessing herself of that help to free agency as there is now to her seizing on the rostrum or the desk; and she is likely to draw, from a permission to plead her cause that way, opposite inferences to what might be wished by those who now grant it.

As to the possibility of her filling with grace and dignity

any such position, we should think those who had seen the great actresses and heard the Quaker preachers of modern times would not doubt that Woman can express publicly the fullness of thought and creation without losing any of the peculiar beauty of her sex. What can pollute and tarnish is to act thus from any motive except that something needs to be said or done. Woman could take part in the processions, the songs, the dances of old religion; no one fancied her delicacy was impaired by appearing in public for such a cause.

As to her home, she is not likely to leave it more than she now does for balls, theaters, meetings for promoting missions, revival meetings, and others to which she flies in hope of an animation for her existence commensurate with what she sees enjoyed by men. Governors of ladies' fairs are no less engrossed by such a charge than the governor of a state by his; presidents of Washingtonian societies no less away from home than presidents of conventions. If men look straitly to it, they will find that unless their lives are domestic, those of the women will not be. A house is no home unless it contain food and fire for the mind as well as for the body. The female Greek of our day is as much in the street as the male to cry, "What news?" We doubt not it was the same in Athens of old. The women, shut out from the market-place, made up for it at the religious festivals. For human beings are not so constituted that they can live without expansion. If they do not get it in one way, they must in another or perish.

As to men's representing women fairly at present, while we hear from men who owe to their wives not only all that is comfortable or graceful but all that is wise in the arrangement of their lives the frequent remark, "You cannot reason with a woman"—when from those of delicacy, nobleness, and poetic culture falls the contemptuous phrase "women and children," and that in no light sally of the hour, but in works intended to give a permanent statement of the best experiences—when not one man in the million, shall I say? no, not in the hundred million, can rise above the belief that Woman was made *for Man*—when such traits as these are daily forced upon the attention, can we feel that Man will always do justice to the interests of Woman? Can we think that he takes a sufficiently discerning and religious view of her office and destiny *ever* to do her justice, except when prompted by sentiment—accidentally or transiently, that is, for the sentiment will vary according to the relations in which he is placed? The lover, the poet, the artist are likely to view her nobly. The father and the philosophy have some chance of liberality; the man of the world, the legislator for expediency none.

Under these circumstances, without attaching importance in themselves to the changes demanded by the champions of Woman, we hail them as signs of the times. We would have every arbitrary barrier thrown down. We would have every path laid open to Woman as freely as to Man. Were this done and a slight temporary fermentation allowed to subside, we should see crystallizations more pure and of more various beauty. We believe the divine energy would pervade nature to a degree unknown in the history of former ages, and that no discordant collision but a ravishing harmony of the spheres would ensue.

Yet then and only then will mankind be ripe for this, when inward and outward freedom for Woman as much as for Man shall be acknowledged as a *right*, not yielded as a concession. As the friend of the Negro assumes that one man cannot by right hold another in bondage, so should the friend of Woman assume that Man cannot by right lay even well-meant restrictions on Woman. If the Negro be a soul, if the woman be a soul, appareled in flesh, to one Master only are they accountable. There is but one law for souls, and if there is to be an interpreter of it, he must come not as man or son of man, but as son of God.

Were thought and feeling once so far elevated that Man should esteem himself the brother and friend, but nowise the lord and tutor, of Woman—were he really bound with her in equal worship—arrangements as to function and employment would be of no consequence. What Woman needs is not as a woman to act or rule, but as a nature to grow, as an intellect to discern, as a soul to live freely and unimpeded to unfold such powers as were given her when we left our common home. If fewer talents were given her, yet if allowed the free and full employment of these, so that she may render back to the giver his own with usury, she will not complain; nay, I dare to say she will bless and rejoice in her earthly birthplace, her earthly lot. Let us consider what obstructions impede this good era, and what signs give reason to hope that it draws near.

I was talking on this subject with Miranda, a woman, who, if any in the world could, might speak without heat and bitterness of the position of her sex. Her father was a man who cherished no sentimental reverence for Woman, but a firm belief in the equality of the sexes. She was his eldest child, and came to him at an age when he needed a companion. From the time she could speak and go alone, he addressed her not as a plaything but as a living mind. Among the few verses he ever wrote was a copy addressed to this child, when the first locks were cut from her head; and the reverence expressed on this occasion for that cherished head, he never belied. It was to him the temple of immortal intellect. He respected his child, however, too much to be an indulgent parent. He called on her for clear judgment, for courage, for honor and fidelity; in short, for such virtues as he knew. In so far as he possessed the keys to the wonders of this universe, he allowed free use of them to her, and by the incentive of a high expectation he forbade, so far as possible, that she should let the privilege lie idle.

Thus this child was early led to feel herself a child of the spirit. She took her place easily not only in the world of organized being, but in the world of mind. A dignified sense of self-dependence was given as all her portion, and she found it a sure anchor. Herself securely anchored, her relations with others were established with equal security. She was fortunate in a total absence of those charms which might have drawn to her bewildering flatteries, and in a strong electric nature which repelled those who did not belong to her and attracted those who did. With men and women her relations were noble—affectionate without passion, intellectual without coldness. The world was free to her, and she lived freely in it. Outward adversity came and inward conflict, but that faith and self-respect had early been awakened which must always lead at last to an outward serenity and an inward peace.

Of Miranda I had always thought as an example, that the

restraints upon the sex were insuperable only to those who think them so, or who noisily strive to break them. She had taken a course of her own, and no man stood in her way. Many of her acts had been unusual, but excited no uproar. Few helped but none checked her; and the many men who knew her mind and her life showed to her confidence as to a brother, gentleness as to a sister. And not only refined, but very coarse men approved and aided one in whom they saw resolution and clearness of design. Her mind was often the leading one, always effective.

When I talked with her upon these matters and had said very much what I have written, she smilingly replied: "And yet we must admit that I have been fortunate, and this should not be. My good father's early trust gave the first bias, and the rest followed of course. It is true that I have had less outward aid in after years than most women; but that is of little consequence. Religion was early awakened in my soul—a sense that what the soul is capable to ask it must attain, and that though I might be aided and instructed by others, I must depend on myself as the only constant friend. This self-dependence, which was honored in me, is deprecated as a fault in most women. They are taught to learn their rule from without, not to unfold it from within.

"This is the fault of Man, who is still vain, and wishes to be more important to Woman than by right he should be."

"Men have not shown this disposition toward you," I said.

"No, because the position I early was enabled to take was one of self-reliance. And were all women as sure of their wants as I was, the result would be the same. But they are so over-loaded with precepts by guardians who think that nothing is so much to be dreaded for a woman as originality of thought or character, that their minds are impeded by doubts till they lose their chance of fair, free proportions. The difficulty is to get them to the point from which they shall naturally develop self-respect and learn self-help.

"Once I thought that men would help to forward this state of things more than I do now. I saw so many of them wretched in the connections they had formed in weakness and vanity. They seemed so glad to esteem women whenever they could.

" 'The soft arms of affection,' said one of the most discerning spirits, 'will not suffice for me, unless on them I see the steel bracelets of strength.'

"But early I perceived that men never in any extreme of despair wished to be women. On the contrary, they were ever ready to taunt one another at any sign of weakness with,

Art thou not like the women, who—

The passage ends various ways, according to the occasion and rhetoric of the speaker. When they admired any woman, they were inclined to speak of her as 'above her sex.' . . ."

The sexes should not only correspond to and appreciate, but prophesy to one another. In individual instances this happens. Two persons love in one another the future good which they aid one another to unfold. This is imperfectly or rarely done in the general life. Man has gone but little way; now he is waiting to see whether Woman can keep step with him, but instead of calling out like a good brother, "You can do it, if you only think so," or impersonally, "Anyone can do what he tries to do"; he often discourages with schoolboy brag: "Girls can't do that; girls can't play ball." But let anyone defy their taunts, break through and be brave and secure, they rend the air with shouts.

*   *   *

Civilized Europe is still in a transition state about marriage; not only in practice but in thought. It is idle to speak with contempt of the nations where polygamy is an institution or seraglios a custom, while practices far more debasing haunt, well-nigh fill, every city and every town, and so far as union of one with one is believed to be the only pure form of marriage, a great majority of societies and individuals are still doubtful whether the earthly bond must be a meeting of souls, or only supposes a contract of convenience and utility. Were Woman established in the rights of an immortal being, this could not be. She would not in some countries be given away by her father, with scarcely more respect for her feelings than is shown by the Indian chief who sells his daughter for a horse, and beats her if she runs away from her new home. Nor in societies where her choice is left free, would she be perverted by the current of opinion that seizes her, into the belief that she must marry, if it be only to find a protector and a home of her own. Neither would Man, if he thought the connection of permanent importance, form it so lightly. He would not deem it a trifle that he was to enter into the closest relations with another soul, which, if not eternal in themselves, must eternally affect his growth. Neither did he believe Woman capable of friendship, would he by rash haste lose the chance of finding a friend in the person who might probably live half a century by his side. Did love to his mind stretch forth into infinity, he would not miss his chance of its revelations, that he might the sooner rest from his weariness by a bright fireside, and secure a sweet and graceful attendant "devoted to him alone." Were he a step higher, he would not carelessly enter into a relation where he might not be able to do the duty of a friend, as well as a protector from external ill, to the other party, and have a being in his power pining for sympathy, intelligence, and aid that he could not give.

What deep communion, what real intercourse is implied in sharing the joys and cares of parentage, when any degree of equality is admitted between the parties! It is true that in a majority of instances the man looks upon his wife as an adopted child, and places her to the other children in the relation of nurse or governess rather than that of parent. Her influence with them is sure; but she misses the education which should enlighten that influence, by being thus treated. It is the order of nature that children should complete the education, moral and mental, of parents by making them think what is needed for the best culture of human beings, and conquer all faults and impulses that interfere with their giving this to these dear objects who represent the world to them. Father and mother should assist one another to learn what is required for this sublime priesthood of Nature. But for this a religious recognition of equality is required. . . .

*   *   *

The especial genius of Woman I believe to be electrical in movement, intuitive in function, spiritual in tendency. She excels not so easily in classification or recreation, as in an instinctive seizure of causes, and a simple breathing out of what she receives that has the singleness of life, rather than the selecting and energizing of art.

More native is it to her to be the living model of the artist than to set apart from herself any one form in objective reality; more native to inspire and receive the poem than to create it. In so far as soul is in her completely developed, all soul is the same; but in so far as it is modified in her as Woman, it flows, it breathes, it sings, rather than deposits soil or finishes work; and that which is especially feminine flushes in blossom the face of earth, and pervades like air and water all this seeming solid globe, daily renewing and purifying its life. Such may be the especially feminine element spoken of as Femality. But it is no more the order of nature that it should be incarnated pure in any form, than that the masculine energy should exist unmingled with it in any form.

Male and female represent the two sides of the great radical dualism. But in fact they are perpetually passing into one another. Fluid hardens to solid, solid rushes to fluid. There is no wholly masculine man, no purely feminine woman.

History jeers at the attempts of physiologists to bind great original laws by the forms which flow from them. They make a rule; they say from observation what can and cannot be. In vain! Nature provides exceptions to every rule. She sends women to battle, and sets Hercules spinning; she enables women to bear immense burdens, cold, and frost; she enables the man who feels maternal love to nourish his infant like a mother. Of late she plays still gayer pranks. Not only she deprives organizations but organs of a necessary end. She enables people to read with the top of the head and see with the pit of the stomach. Presently she will make a female Newton and a male siren.

Man partakes of the feminine in the Apollo; Woman of the masculine as Minerva.

What I mean by the Muse is that unimpeded clearness of

the intuitive powers, which a perfectly truthful adherence to every admonition of the higher instincts would bring to a finely organized human being. It may appear as prophecy or as poesy. It enabled Cassandra to foresee the results of actions passing round her; the Seeress to behold the true character of the person through the mask of his customary life. (Sometimes she saw a feminine form behind the man, sometimes the reverse.) It enabled the daughter of Linnaeus to see the soul of the flower exhaling from the flower. It gave a man, but a poet-man, the power of which he thus speaks: "Often in my contemplation of nature, radiant intimations and as it were sheaves of light appear before me as to the facts of cosmogony, in which my mind has perhaps taken especial part." He wisely adds, "But it is necessary with earnestness to verify the knowledge we gain by these flashes of light." And none should forget this. Sight must be verified by light before it can deserve the honors of piety and genius. Yet sight comes first, and of this sight of the world of causes, this approximation to the region of primitive motions, women I hold to be especially capable. Even without equal freedom with the other sex, they have already shown themselves so; and should these faculties have free play, I believe they will open new, deeper, and purer sources of joyous inspiration than have as yet refreshed the earth.

Let us be wise, and not impede the soul. Let her work as she will. Let us have one creative energy, one incessant revelation. Let it take what form it will, and let us not bind it by the past to man or woman, black or white. Jove sprang from Rhea, Pallas from Jove. So let it be.

If it has been the tendency of these remarks to call Woman rather to the Minerva side—if I, unlike the more generous writer, have spoken from society no less than the soul—let it be pardoned! It is love that has caused this—love for many incarcerated souls that might be freed could the idea of religious self-dependence be established in them, could the weakening habit of dependence on others be broken up.

*   *   *

It is therefore that I would have Woman lay aside all thought, such as she habitually cherishes, of being taught and led by men. I would have her, like the Indian girl, dedicate herself to the Sun, the Sun of Truth, and go nowhere if his beams did not make clear the path. I would have her free from compromise, from complaisance, from helplessness, because I would have her good enough and strong enough to love one and all beings, from the fullness, not the poverty of being.

Men as at present instructed will not help this work, because they also are under the slavery of habit. I have seen with delight their poetic impulses. A sister is the fairest ideal, and how nobly Wordsworth and even Byron have written of a sister!

There is no sweeter sight than to see a father with his little daughter. Very vulgar men become refined to the eye when leading a little girl by the hand. At that moment, the right relation between the sexes seems established, and you feel as if the man would aid in the noblest purpose, if you ask him in behalf of his little daughter. Once, two fine figures stood before me thus. The father of very intellectual aspect, his falcon eye softened by affection as he looked down on his fair child; she the image of himself, only more graceful and brilliant in expression. I was reminded of Southey's Kehama; when, lo, the dream was rudely broken! They were talking of education, and he said:

"I shall not have Maria brought too forward. If she knows too much, she will never find a husband; superior women hardly ever can."

"Surely," said his wife with a blush, "you wish Maria to be as good and wise as she can, whether it will help her to marriage or not."

"No," he persisted, "I want her to have a sphere and a home, and someone to protect her when I am gone."

It was a trifling incident, but made a deep impression. I felt that the holiest relations fail to instruct the unprepared and perverted mind. If this man indeed could have looked at it on the other side, he was the last that would have been willing to have been taken himself for the home and protection he could give, but would have been much more likely to repeat the tale of Alcibiades with his phials.

But men do *not* look at both sides, and women must leave off asking them and being influenced by them, but retire within themselves, and explore the groundwork of life till they find their peculiar secret. Then, when they come forth again, renovated and baptized, they will know how to turn all dross to gold, and will be rich and free though they live in a hut, tranquil if in a crowd. Then their sweet singing shall not be from passionate impulse, but the lyrical overflow of a divine rapture, and a new music shall be evolved from this many-chorded world.

Grant her, then, for a while the armor and the javelin. Let her put from her the press of other minds, and meditate in virgin loneliness. The same idea shall reappear in due time as Muse, or Ceres, the all-kindly, patient Earth Spirit.

*   *   *

I believe that at present women are the best helpers of one another.

Let them think, let them act, till they know what they need.

We only ask of men to remove arbitrary barriers. Some would like to do more. But I believe it needs that Woman show herself in her native dignity to teach them how to aid her; their minds are so encumbered by tradition.

When Lord Edward Fitzgerald traveled with the Indians, his manly heart obliged him at once to take the packs from the squaws and carry them. But we do not read that the red men followed his example, though they are ready enough to carry the pack of the white woman, because she seems to them a superior being.

Let Woman appear in the mild majesty of Ceres, and rudest churls will be willing to learn from her.

You ask: what use will she make of liberty, when she has so long been sustained and restrained?

I answer: in the first place this will not be suddenly given. I read yesterday a debate of this year on the subject of enlarging women's rights over property. It was a leaf from the classbook that is preparing for the needed instruction. The men learned visibly as they spoke. The champions of Woman saw the fallacy of arguments on the opposite side, and were startled by their own convictions. With their wives at home, and the readers of the paper, it was the same. And so the stream flows on; thought urging action, and action leading to the evolution of still better thought.

But were this freedom to come suddenly, I have no fear of the consequences. Individuals might commit excesses, but there is not only in the sex a reverence for decorums and limits inherited and enhanced from generation to generation, which many years of other life could not efface, but a native love in Woman, as Woman, of proportion, of "the simple art of not too much"—a Greek moderation which would create immediately a restraining party, the natural legislators and instructors of the rest, and would gradually establish such rules as are needed to guard without impeding life.

The Graces would lead the choral dance, and teach the rest to regulate their steps to the measure of beauty.

But if you ask me what offices they may fill, I reply—any. I do not care what case you put; let them be sea-captains, if you will. I do not doubt there are women well fitted for such an office, and if so, I should be as glad to see them in it....

I think women need especially at this juncture a much greater range of occupation than they have, to rouse their latent powers. A party of travelers lately visited a lonely hut on a mountain. There they found an old woman, who told them she and her husband had lived their forty years. "Why," they said, "did you choose so barren a spot?" She did not know; "*it was the man's notion.*"

And during forty years she had been content to act, without knowing why, upon the "man's notion." I would not have it so.

In families that I know, some little girls like to saw wood, others to use carpenters' tools. Where these tastes are indulged, cheerfulness and good-humor are promoted. Where they are forbidden, because "such things are not proper for girls," they grow sullen and mischievous.

Fourier had observed these wants of women, as no one can fail to do who watches the desires of little girls or knows the ennui that haunts grown women, except where they make to themselves a serene little world by art of some kind. He therefore, in proposing a great variety of employments in manufactures or the care of plants and animals, allows for one third of women as likely to have a taste for masculine pursuits, one third of men for feminine.

Who does not observe the immediate glow and serenity that is diffused over the life of women before restless or fretful by engaging in gardening, building, or the lowest department of art? Here is something that is not routine, something that draws forth life towards the infinite.

I have no doubt, however, that a large proportion of women would give themselves to the same employments as now, because there are circumstances that must lead them. Mothers will delight to make the nest soft and warm. Nature would take care of that; no need to clip the wings of any bird that wants to soar and sing, or finds in itself the strength of pinion for a migratory flight unusual to its kind. The difference would be that *all* need not be constrained to employments for which *some* are unfit.

I have urged upon the sex self-subsistence in its two forms of self-reliance and self-impulse, because I believe them to be the needed means of the present juncture.

I have urged on Woman independence of Man, not that I do not think the sexes mutually needed by one another, but because in Woman this fact has led to an excessive devotion which has cooled love, degraded marriage, and prevented either sex from being what it should be to itself or the other.

I wish Woman to live *first* for God's sake. Then she will not make an imperfect man her god, and thus sink to idolatry. Then she will not take what is not fit for her from a sense of weakness and poverty. Then if she finds what she needs in Man embodied, she will know how to love and be worthy of being loved.

By being more a soul she will not be less Woman, for nature is perfected through spirit.

Now there is no woman, only an overgrown child.

That her hand may be given with dignity, she must be able to stand alone. I wish to see men and women capable of such relations as are depicted by Landor in his *Pericles and Aspasia*, where grace is the natural garb of strength, and the affections are calm, because deep. The softness is that of a firm tissue, as when

> *The gods approve*
> *The depth, but not the tumult of the soul,*
> *A fervent, not ungovernable love.*

A profound thinker has said, "No married woman can represent the female world, for she belongs to her husband. The idea of Woman must be represented by a virgin."

But that is the very fault of marriage and of the present relation between the sexes, that the woman *does* belong to the man instead of forming a whole with him. Were it otherwise, there would be no such limitation to the thought.

Woman, self-centered, would never be absorbed by any relation; it would be only an experience to her as to man. It is a vulgar error that love, *a* love, to Woman is her whole existence; she also is born for Truth and Love in their universal energy. Would she but assume her inheritance, Mary would not be the only virgin mother.

And will not she soon appear? The woman who shall vindicate their birthright for all women; who shall teach them what to claim, and how to use what they obtain? Shall not her name be for her era Victoria, for her country and life Virginia? Yet predictions are rash; she herself must teach us to give her the fitting name.

An idea not unknown to ancient times has of late been revived, that in the metamorphoses of life the soul assumes the form first of Man, then of Woman, and takes the chances and reaps the benefits of either lot. Why then, say some, lay such emphasis on the rights or needs of Woman? What she wins not as Woman will come to her as Man.

That makes no difference. It is not Woman, but the law of right, the law of growth that speaks in us and demands the perfection of each being in its kind—apple as apple, Woman as Woman. Without adopting your theory, I know that I, a daughter, live through the life of Man; but what concerns me now is that my life be a beautiful, powerful, in a word, a complete life in its kind. Had I but one more moment to live I must wish the same.

Suppose at the end of your cycle, your great world-year, all will be completed whether I exert myself or not (and the supposition is *false*—but suppose it true), am I to be indifferent about it? Not so! I must beat my own pulse true in the heart of the world; for *that* is virtue, excellence, health.

Thou, Lord of Day, didst leave us tonight so calmly glorious, not dismayed that cold winter is coming, not postponing thy beneficence to the fruitful summer! Thou didst smile on thy day's work when it was done, and adorn thy down-going as thy up-rising, for thou art loyal, and it is thy nature to give life, if thou canst, and shine at all events!

I stand in the sunny noon of life. Objects no longer glitter in the dews of morning, neither are yet softened by the shadows of evening. Every spot is seen, every chasm revealed. Climbing the dusty hill, some fair effigies that once stood for symbols of human destiny have been broken; those I still have with me show defects in this broad light. Yet enough is left, even by experience, to point distinctly to the glories of that destiny; faint but not to be mistaken streaks of the future day. I can say with the bard,

> *Though many have suffered shipwreck, still beat noble hearts.*

Always the soul says to us all, cherish your best hopes as a faith, and abide by them in action. Such shall be the effectual fervent means to their fulfillment:

For the Power to whom we bow
Has given its pledge that, if not now,
They of pure and steadfast mind,
By faith exalted, truth refined,
Shall *hear all music loud and clear,*
Whose first notes they ventured here.
Then fear not thou to wind the horn,
Though elf and gnome thy courage scorn;
Ask for the castle's King and Queen;
Though rabble rout may rush between,
Beat thee senseless to the ground,
In the dark beset thee round;
Persist to ask, and it will come;
Seek not for rest in humbler home;
So shalt thou see, what few have seen,
The palace home of King and Queen.

November 15, 1844

"The Women of Scotland to the Free Women of the United States of America"

THE NORTH STAR, February 11, 1848

Frederick Douglass, the ex-slave who became one of the leaders of the abolition movement, edited a newspaper called THE NORTH STAR from 1847 to 1864. The following article illustrates the transatlantic nature of the slavery issue as well as its close association with religion. This anonymous author calls upon women in the United States—in the slave as well as the free states— to take a stand against slavery. But since southern postmasters were refusing to handle abolitionist literature by the 1840s, it is doubtful that many southern women read this piece, or any others that appeared in periodicals denouncing slavery.

Dear Sisters: Enjoying freedom ourselves, our desire is, that its blessings should be extended to every member of the human family. In your country there are three millions of our fellow-mortals, descended from the same Parent as ourselves, in whose veins run the same blood as in our own—whose visages bear the same divine impress—whose hearts are susceptible of the same impulses—whose souls must stand before the same judgment-seat, and inhabit the same eternity as our own— who, notwithstanding their being under a Government, the

Source: "The Women of Scotland to the Free Women of the United States of America," *The North Star* 1, no. 7 (11 Feb. 1848).

Frederick Douglass. *(Courtesy: Library of Congress)*

fundamental declaration of whose Constitution is, "That all are born free and equal," have in disregard of any principle of nature and religion, been robbed of their most sacred rights— doomed by the laws of your country to a perpetual and degrading bondage—regarded as beasts of burden—bought and sold as articles of merchandise—all the ties of social life disregarded—the husband and wife, the parent and the child, subject to be for ever separated—deprived of every means of instruction, intellectual and moral—and, above all, denuded of that liberty which is the right of every human being breathing the vital air.

We ask you to pause and reflect on this unseemly and wicked state of things; emancipate yourself from that bondage of custom, or prejudice, or interest, under which you may be laboring; contemplate the horrors of the slave system with an open and candid mind; realize as far as you can, an adequate conception of the realities of this evil; ascertain in what way you stand connected with it; and, looking at that connection in the light of a final reckoning, decide at once whether Slavery is in future to count upon you as friends or foes. Our religion teaches that God is the Father of us all, and that freedom is the sacred birthright of all his children. We, therefore, protest against any member of this family robbing any other of this inalienable gift, and call upon all who have escaped the horrors of bondage to break these fetters, and let the oppressed go free.

It grieves us to learn that not a few of you, who professedly recognize the Christian religion as the rule of life, are actually identified with the slave system of your country, living in the very midst of it, surrounded by those whom God has endowed with the same gifts as yourselves, and who, you cannot deny, are brothers and sisters of that great family to which you belong.—They are kept in bondage for your sakes; they are deprived of intellectual, moral and religious culture, that they may the better serve your selfish purposes. There is no necessity impelling you to hold longer over them the rod of the oppressor; you may, if you choose, wash your hands, at once clean of this evil. Do not imagine that because you have been born and educated in the midst of Slavery, that you are guiltless, or at least comparatively innocent, however much these unhappy circumstances may have tended to blunt your moral sensibilities, or to mitigate your guilt when you lived (if it were possible so to live) in ignorance of your criminality; be assured that now, when your attention has been called in the sinfulness of your position, that if you have left in your breasts one single vestige of that moral preception which distinguishes our nature, so long as you stand in any degree identified with Slavery, that you are unmitigated transgressors of the immutable laws of God's moral government.

We urge you once more humbly to review the principles of the Christian religion. Ponder well that great commandment which included all others, "Love the Lord thy God with all thy heart, and they neighbor as thyself,"—learn again the spirit of that golden maxim, "Do unto others as ye would they should do unto you." Are you willing to change conditions with these who are held in bondage by you, or for you? Are you willing to entrust your future happiness to the caprice of the taskmaster—at his will, to be torn from your husband or father, your child or sister, and separated forever? Are you prepared to abandon all your right; civil and religious—to be deprived of every means of instruction—to be herded as cattle are—sold at the auction block to the highest bidder—your persons to be flogged, abused, or destroyed as best suits the purpose of those into whose hands you may fall? If not, then love your neighbor as yourselves, do unto others as ye would they should do unto you—or at once honestly renounce the professed service of a Master whom you are not willing to obey;—far better for yourselves, and for the cause of suffering humanity, that you boldly renounce a religion which lays you under restrictions to that which you are resolved not to submit, than that you should deceive the world and your own selves by attempting to do what never can be done—serve both God and Mammon. . . .

There are in your country a large class, who, not being actually involved in the slave system, imagine that they occupy a neutral position, and are therefore free from the charge of supporting slavery. To such, we would say, between right and wrong there is no neutral ground. "He who is not with us is against us," is the language of One who always spoke the truth; if you are not protesting against slavery, if you have not repudiated the fellowship of those who live by its existence, then, according to the statement of Jesus, you are not with us, but with those who are against us. There can be no greater or more fatal error than to imagine, that slavery depends for its existence upon the holders of slaves; it could not exist a year if left solely to depend upon them for support; they are the mere executors of the religious sentiment of your country on this matter, and would be powerless under a correct public opinion. Your pro-slavery churches are "the Bulwarks of Slavery;" they are giving their mighty influence to perpetuate the present state of things; they have refrained from declaring the criminality of man attempting to hold property in his fellow man:— nay, they defend such a state of things, as perfectly consistent with the precepts and spirit of Christianity. They have received into their most intimate fellowship the slaveholders of your land, and thus endorsed the whole system as good; they are not with us, but against us. The Church has, in every age and in every country, been the most powerful regulator of public sentiment, inasmuch as it deals with the religious feelings of the people; but the church is made up of its individual members, so its influence is the combination of theirs. If your influence, then, has been thrown into the common stock of any church, where slavery and its supporters are not the subjects of separation and unqualified condemnation, are you free from the charge of perpetuating this evil and prolonging its horrors? We would remind you that our guilt, in connection with any system of iniquity, can only be measured by the amount of influence we possess.—The more reputedly good men and women are, the more dangerous do they become, when they sanction that which is evil; slavery reaps a greater harvest from the silence of such, than from the efforts of all the slaveholders in your land. Let your churches give forth an unqualified condemnation of this system, let your ministers fearlessly declare from their pulpits its true character, and slavery with its attendant evils, will speedily disappear; but if they persist in perpetuating this fearful delusion, iniquity will wax stronger and stronger, till those virtues which are the only guarantee of your country's preservation, shall be blotted out.

We would say, take decided action; let your creed be, no compromise with slavery—no communion with slaveholders; if the church to which you belong will not stand forth in vindication of the rights of your colored countrymen, then be faithful to your religion—"Come out of her my people, that ye partake not of her sins, and that ye receive not of her plagues."

To that small, but ever increasing class, who, for a long series of years have, amid scorn and persecution, been devoting their entire energies to the work of your country's emancipation, we look with feelings of the deepest sympathy and the fondest hope; we have not been inattentive observers of the self-sacrificing course of William Lloyd Garrison and his devoted compeers. The countless attempts made by the pro-slavery men of your land to blast their reputation and the unbounded confidence placed in them by your colored population, is to our minds conclusive evidence of their exalted worth, of their growing success, and of our own bounden duty to cheer and aid them on by every means in our power.

"Address of Anti-Slavery Women of Western New York"

THE NORTH STAR, March 31, 1848

When women of the 1830s and 1840s were discouraged from participating along with men in abolitionist societies, they formed their own. Some men, like Frederick Douglass, were sympathetic and supportive, and his newspaper often carried articles such as the following. This regional society was one of many that sprang up in the Northeast and the Midwest. As this article demonstrates, reform-minded women were answering the feminist call to public action in worthy causes, but they were careful not to flout accepted notions of woman's proper sphere. Raising money by holding sewing circles was hardly radical behavior.

Under a deep and abiding impression of the duty we owe to God and our fellow beings, the Anti-Slavery women of Rochester feel constrained to continue to persevere in their efforts for the oppressed and suffering bondmen who still remain toiling unrequited in the Southern prison house. We are frequently brought painfully to remember that not only is their labor wrested from them unremunerated; not only do they suffer from intense hunger and cold; not only are the females, our SIS-TERS, subjected to the cruel and passionate outrages of their

Source: "Address of Anti-Slavery Women of Western New York," *The North Star* 1, no. 14 (31 Mar. 1848).

tyrannical masters and overseers; but there are daily instances of sundering the dearest ties in nature, thus separating them forever. And can we expect anything better—can we look for benevolence or fine feelings from a system so foul and fiendish as slavery! It would be unreasonable, because "a corrupt tree cannot bring forth good fruit." Therefore, knowing that without associative action we cannot render efficient aid to this holy cause, we affectionately invite the co-operation of the citizens of Rochester and the public generally. We ask them to bear in mind the injunctions of Jesus, "All things whatsoever ye would men should do to you, do ye even so to them." Remember, also, the beautiful parable in which he calls our attention to the sick and to those who are in prison, and concludes by the forcible assertion, "Inasmuch as ye have done it to one of the least of these my brethren, ye have done it unto me." We feel assured all that have hearts to feel, and are careful to attend to the monitions of conscience—all who are determined to live for the good of our race, instead of devoting all their time to their own personal ease—all who feel bound to improve the precious time allotted to them here, by promoting as much as possible the cause of truth and righteousness in the earth, will come forward in the work of laboring to banish forever the demon of slavery from our land; and in so doing, instead of an example of corruption and wickedness, we should be a "light to the world."

We hope no one will feel too poor, nor any too rich, to enlist in this holy cause. The Christian's influence, in whatever situation, is always salutary, and will certainly produce its good effects. We ask for the aid of men and of women;—we call on the old and the young, the farmer, the mechanic, and the merchant. We ask all and every one to give us their help; to devote what they can spare, either of money or of the fruits of their labor, to the work of restoring men and women to themselves, to their manhood, to the rights and blessings with which they were endowed by our Creator.

For this object, we propose holding a Fair in December next. We ask the females in the adjoining towns and country around us, to get up sewing circles, and prepare such articles as will be most saleable, and to come, furnish tables, give us their company, and help us, not only in selling those things thus prepared, but in convincing the public mind of the necessity of our perseverance and fidelity, and thus be helpers in hastening the day of emancipation.

"Woman"

THE NORTH STAR, May 26, 1848

The following essay appeared less than a month be-
fore the Seneca Falls Convention. In this lengthy selec-
tion from the WASHINGTON COUNTY JOURNAL,
reprinted in THE NORTH STAR, woman's special
qualities are praised, and examples of famous women
from history are used to demonstrate women's capabili-
ties, but the piece is conservative in tone. It should be
contrasted to Elizabeth Cady Stanton's bold statement
on a woman's rightful place in a male-dominated soci-
ety in her speech to the New York legislature, on pages
196–212 of this volume.

WOMAN.

——"Is woman's lovely frame
A gemless casket, fitted not to claim
The eye's devotion?
Though she permits your rougher hand to bear
The rod of power—your loftier brow to wear
The glittering badge of sovereignty, she still
Directs, unseen, the sceptre at her will,
Wisdom may act, determine, or approve,
Still the prime mover is and must be love."

To expatiate upon the social condition of woman, and to
exhibit many traits in the female character, is a lofty, touching,
and lovely theme. It is lofty, as it opens a field for the investiga-

Source: "Woman," *The North Star* 1, no. 22 (26 May 1848).

tion of all the nobler qualities of the human mind. It is touching and lovely, as in them are exhibited the emotions of the heart, the moving springs that prompt to deeds of charity and mercy. In them, we discover the source of the tender sensibilities and moral affections. While panegyric sinks before the names of Hemans, Sigourney, and many others made immortal by their literary productions, it may not be uninteresting to notice some of the relations incident to them as social beings, and which are important to them, either as securing their happiness or misery.

Woman in our social compact occupies a position, apparently, so elevated, so merited, and so firmly established, that it may hardly be thought, by some, to furnish a field of sufficient interest to attract our attention, or demand a flourish of the pen. If it is true, that the social relations, in this our beloved land, secure to woman all the privileges and rights which Heaven designed should fall to her lot, she now participates, what has required centuries to effect. The benign influences that now cluster around her path, are the result of that expansion of intellect, and that development of the moral attributes, that ages alone produced. The various causes, that combined to work the vast changes, the benefit of which she now experiences, are found in revelation—have been multiplied by the progress of science—owe their origin to the light of Christianity, and present an interesting feature of the annals of the past. But it is not true, that even in our land of "warm hearts and open hands," she receives the regards her natural abilities and the important position she occupies demand. She moves within a sphere, the radiating influences of which are to be pure, lovely, holy, or of the most debasing character, proportionate to the nature of the fountain from whence they spring. She moulds each successive generation. She impresses the youthful mind with a signet that time cannot efface—that reaches through and takes a firm hold of immortality,

> "Then say to mothers, what a holy charge
> Is theirs; with what a kingly power their love
> Might rule the fountain of the new-born intellect."

Art may embellish, rigid science may expand and expose to view the hidden treasures of the mind; but 'tis left to the soft pencilings of the gifted mother's hand, to impress on the heart in living characters, the attribute to be prized above all others, virtue. If such, then, be her heavenly calling, how lovely, how sacred her mission! She is not a "gemless casket." The field of her labor is as broad as time itself, and as varied as her eccentricities of character. Blest with a versatility of genius by nature—equal to or surpassing that of her self-created lord—it is soon developed when brought within the influence of civilization, and burnished by the spirit of refinement. There is a chord running through society, touched by the magic of her hand, whose vibrations every heart can feel. Do we turn to the pages of antiquity to learn her early history, we there often find the impress of her lovely character.—In the most ancient record to which we have access, we find that woman was created equal with man, or that in the creation, the term *man* is to be taken in its generic sense, as comprehending both sexes, and, for reasons therein given, we find the following declaration, "That man shall leave his father and mother, and shall cleave unto his wife, and they shall be one flesh," which shows in what light the Creator of the human family regarded the marital obligations, and the equality of the sexes. And that woman, at an early day, exercised an influence over man, is strikingly exhibited in the case of Adam and Eve. And as an evidence of the tenacity of female friendship, we have an early example in the wife of Cain. For when God had pronounced sentence of banishment upon Cain, and put a mark upon him, his wife endured with meekness the mortifying sentence; and cheerfully with him suffered the penalty.

ADAH.—"Cain, thou hast heard we must go forth, I am
　　　　ready;
　　　So shall our children be. I will bear Enoch,
　　　And you his sister. Ere the sun declines,
　　　Let us depart, nor walk the wilderness
　　　Under the cloud of night. Nay, speak to me,
　　　To me—thine own.

CAIN—Leave me!
ADAH—Why, all have left thee!
CAIN—And wherefore lingerest thou? Dost thou not fear
    To dwell with one who hath done this?
ADAH—   I fear
    Nothing except to leave thee, much as I
    Shrink from the deed that leaves thee brotherless.
    ————My office is
    Henceforth to dry up tears, not to shed them,
    But yet, of all who mourn, none mourn like me;
    Now, Cain, I will divide thy burden with thee.
CAIN—Eastward from Eden will we take our way;
    'Tis the most desolate, and suits my steps."

And if woman, by reason of partaking of the forbidden fruit, subjected herself to the penalty of having her sorrows increased, and that man should rule over her—Christianity teaches us that this sway should not be of a despotic and tyrannical nature, but one of kindness, being interested for her welfare and the promotion of her happiness. In early history, though doomed to suffer, through the neglect of man, or in consequence of ignorance, barbarism, and a debased state of society, yet as the glittering diamond discovers itself in the dark, so has she, by the brilliant display of intellect, often burst the surrounding gloom and excited the admiration of the world.

"How fine and marvellous the subtle intellect is,
Beauty's Creator! it adorns the body
And lights it like a star. It shines
forever; and like a watch-tower
To the infidel, shows there is a land to come."

Her countenance, expressive with the artless smile that wins the heart—graceful and elastic in her movements—gentle and confiding in her bearing, barbarism itself, through her entreaty, sinks to pity, and melts to tender sympathy. At her nod, the savage incantations cease, the kindling flame is quenched, the avenger's hand is stayed, and innocence, unoutraged, goes trailing on her way. If in the savage or hunter state, the position assigned her is that of a menial slave—a beast of burden—and her beauty, her loveliness, constitute the basis of her value; relatively, she is as highly prized and as much appreciated by her wild untutored lord, as she is by her enlightened though hardly less severe task-master, in a state where art and science have embellished, and brought into lively exercise, powers, alike possessed by her in nature, differing perhaps in degree, whether born, where

> "The shuddering tenant of the frigid zone,
> Boldly proclaims the happiest spot his own;
> Extols the treasures of his stormy seas,
> And his long nights of revelry and ease."

Or where

> "The naked negro panting at the line,
> Boasts of his golden sands and palmy wine;
> Basks in the glare, or stems the tepid wave,
> And thanks his gods for all the good they gave."

Appreciation, then, in the savage or civilized state, without the ability and the disposition to elevate, is the same. Relatively, there is but little difference in the social relations—as between the sexes—in any age. By the savage, she is prized for possessing qualities that shall most and best conduce to his comfort and happiness. Among enlightened, she is scarcely prized for anything more or less. If in enlightened society, she moves in a more exalted sphere—'tis even so with the opposite sex.

The gradual progress of civilization and refinement, slowly elevated woman from her original situation, to a position more congenial to her character and genius. No sooner did the light of science begin to dispel the darkness of barbarism, which had for ages brooded over the earth with the blackness of midnight, and begin to exert its genial influence over the human mind, enervated for centuries by superstition and ignorance, than woman, with man, released from mental bondage, acquires a position in society more appropriate and important. Men of enlightened minds begin to esteem her for her many virtues, and admire her lovely character. Many were deified and venerated equally with the male deities, which indicates how much the sex by them was prized. Still, her condition in Greece, the cradle of European intellect and civilization, show that, even when Greece was at the zenith of her refinement and glory, woman had not acquired that station in society which her genius peculiarly fitted. By the forced and artificial institutions of Sparta, she was taught to cultivate and admire those qualities which belong exclusively to the masculine sex—to wrestle, almost in a state of nudity, promiscuously with men; to rejoice over the death of her son if he fell gloriously in battle; to practise the crime of infanticide upon her too feeble offspring, and to sacrifice every feminine quality to the military success of the republic.

At Athens, the birth place of taste and refinement, the value of intellectual female society was better acknowledged and felt. But there, usage and custom, more despotic and more tyrannical than law, exacted of virtuous and ingenuous woman a life of seclusion.—Hence, but few attained to much distinction; and they highly accomplished, celebrated by poets, courted by philosophers and princes, sustaining doubtful characters, ruled the world of taste, beauty, and refinement, and usurped among the spiritual and beauty loving Greeks those regards that belong to purity and virtue alone.

It remains then, for Civilization and Christianity combined to give her that high position evidently designed by God, and to secure to her the full fruition of all the immunities that her natural capacities and the advantages of civilization claim for her. The more expanded her intellect—the purer her virtue—the severer her chastity—the more exalted will be her position, the more powerful the influence she will exert over man. She being an object of man's solicitude, the more he associates with her, the more will his character assimilate itself to hers. 'Tis a principle in morals, no less true than its consequences are terrible or commendable, that man assimilates himself to the character of the object he loves or worships. If he admires the contentious and brawling woman, he will soon become a war-like and villanous man. If he admires that feature of the female character which is symbolical of the moral attributes, virtue, chastity, love, and everything that gives life and energy to god-like acts, the hard, unmalleable parts of his moral fabric become softened, and soon his whole character is changed. His lion-like ferocity is subdued. His gross nature is soon refined, and as by magic, the hard-hearted, hard-fisted man, the groveling, niggardly cormorant becomes the polished gentleman.

Does the world of letters, or the vast field of human science, present to the gifted mind allurements that successively draw into deep exercise every element of the intellectual combination, the literary conflict won, the mystic problem solved, the charm that held the mind, thus taxed to its extremest stretch, now seeks repose. And where can it be found, but with the sublime, the heaven-born influences that alone can be enjoyed where the social relations are kept pure and sacred. 'Tis there that the mental or physical labor looks for that enjoyment which nowhere else can be found. 'Tis there that the exhausted mind is ready to acknowledge the truth, that though

> "Wisdom may act, determine, or approve,
> Still the prime mover is and must be love."

It matters little whether we comtemplate Palmyra's proud and gifted queen, issuing from her lofty gates upon the plains that surround that ancient but gorgeous city, with her countless legions enlisted in her cause "to the death," through the magic of her queenly bearing—a token of her resistless sway—to mingle in bloody carnage, hand to hand with her enemies; or at her bidding, burst from the conflict, to seek protection from the sanguine field within the city's walls; or whether we listen to the wisdom and power of her counsels, when in the midst of her assembled ministers of State, men gifted in all the learning of their time, and having much experience, she astounds them with the vastness of her mighty projects, elicits their profound attention by the beauties and reasonableness of her logic; and in the originality of her designs alike excites their wonder and admiration. In speechless amazement they listen till the pleasure of thought becomes painful, till they can no longer restrain their emotions, and then, in accents of merited applause, simultaneously break out with, "Long live our matchless Zenobia!"

It matters little, whether we contemplate the long celebrated Cleopatra, by her beauty, her fascinations, subjecting to her sway the conqueror of a world, a Cæsar, one of the greatest warriors of which history speaks, or when summoned to the Judgment Hall to receive sentence of expatriation or death— we behold her, by artifice, subvert the channels of justice, win to her favor and excite the admiration and love of her judge— forgetful of other martial obligations—and obtain the half an empire. If we are surprised that she could so hold enslaved the affections of an Anthony, a Triumvir of the Roman Empire, as that he should stab himself on hearing of her death, we can hardly be less astonished to witness her giving audience, at the same time, to seven different nations, speaking their languages as fluently as her own. Without multiplying examples, I say it matters little in what aspect we view the mighty influences these heroines; centuries past, exerted over the destinies of men and empires. On either hand we see their fearful power. In it we recognize those remarkable traits, often strikingly exhibited in the female character, which commend them to us as objects worthy our profound regard and deep solicitude, which furnishes evidence that rather militates against the somewhat accredited doctrine, that "man is the lord of creation," and evidence that the term man, when used in this connection, is to be taken in its generic sense; and evidence, too, that, in this universal administration, neither one could with propriety say to the other, "I have no need of thee." If then, the deduction drawn be true, and is, that it would be hazardous to annihilate from the face of the earth either species of the human family, the conclusion follows that the relations between the two are and must be of a deeply interesting character; that these relations should be fostered with the greatest care, the interests of each should ever be regarded as the mutual interest of both. That as they are concomitants of the physical world, only moving in different spheres, and are each, by their immortality, equally allied to the spiritual existence; their physical being should be nurtured, educated, exercised, differing only as to the orbits in which they move; while their spiritual being should be equally subject to and receive the same discipline. Then away with the idea, that after man, woman was created, to pander to his wants, his passions, appetite and lust. Woman was born to a noble, more exalted, holier calling. And of that day, when she shall fully enjoy the high behests that her calling merits, we may well say,

> "Sweet day, so pure, so calm, so bright,
> The bridal of the earth and sky."

Though, possibly, her mind may not be so strong and penetrating as that of man, yet, doubtless, she possesses a greater versatility of genius. While the one is cumbrous and sluggish in its movements, and like time moves slowly on, the other, with its natural elasticity and quickness of apprehension, grasps subject after subject in quick succession.

Is she desirous of figuring in the world of letters, she soon attains to literary distinction. Does she crave her minstrelsy, the muse, at her bidding, adds numbers to her song. By her frequent investigations of developments in solid science, she soon merits more solemn praise. If like man, she is subject to passion, while the former feels but little compunction of conscience for his crime, she, like Althea, kills herself in grief. Patient, enduring, she is scarcely less irresistible than man in the accomplishment of any object. That she possesses a large share of man's affections, in every age of the world, is now too well understood to require further argumentative support. . . .

By nature, she is fitted to occupy a position as elevated and dignified as her self-created master. And though she is often treated by him as his drudge, or a convenient piece of household furniture, 'tis but a striking evidence of his mental imbecility and moral depravity. It argues nothing against her being as intellectual as himself, or that she is not admirably calculated to administer to his physical pleasures and to his mental entertainment—to check the outbreakings of his more violent nature—to soften the too hard features of his sterner character and cultivate the more tender feelings of his soul, and to exert upon him that pacifying influence without which he had been a brute.

PART
2

THE SENECA FALLS CONVENTION OF 1848

Eighty Years and More (1898)

Elizabeth Cady Stanton

When she was eighty-three, Elizabeth Cady Stanton wrote her autobiography, Eighty Years and More, *published in 1898. Advancing years had not slowed her work in the cause of women's rights, and she continued her lifelong crusade for women's equality. She also wrote the controversial* Woman's Bible, *a feminist interpretation of the Scriptures, in two volumes, published in 1895 and 1898. In this excerpt from her autobiography she recalls her awakening to women's rights at the London Anti-Slavery Convention of 1840, and the planning and proceedings of the 1848 convention. Looking back on that convention fifty years later, her most vivid memories are the criticism it inspired, rather than the radicalism of its goals.*

Our chief object in visiting England at this time was to attend the World's Anti-slavery Convention, to meet June 12, 1840, in Freemasons' Hall, London. Delegates from all the anti-slavery societies of civilized nations were invited, yet, when they arrived, those representing associations of women were rejected. Though women were members of the National Anti-slavery Society, accustomed to speak and vote in all its conventions, and to take an equally active part with men in the whole anti-slavery struggle, and were there as delegates from

Source: Elizabeth Cady Stanton, *Eighty Years and More: Reminiscences, 1815–1897* (New York, 1898; reprint, New York, 1971).

associations of men and women, as well as those distinctively of their own sex, yet all alike were rejected because they were women. Women, according to English prejudices at that time, were excluded by Scriptural texts from sharing equal dignity and authority with men in all reform associations; hence it was to English minds pre-eminently unfitting that women should be admitted as equal members to a World's Convention. The question was hotly debated through an entire day. My husband made a very eloquent speech in favor of admitting the women delegates.

When we consider that Lady Byron, Anna Jameson, Mary Howitt, Mrs. Hugo Reid, Elizabeth Fry, Amelia Opie, Ann Green Phillips, Lucretia Mott, and many remarkable women, speakers and leaders in the Society of Friends, were all compelled to listen in silence to the masculine platitudes on woman's sphere, one may form some idea of the indignation of unprejudiced friends, and especially that of such women as Lydia Maria Child, Maria Chapman, Deborah Weston, Angelina and Sarah Grimké, and Abby Kelly, who were impatiently waiting and watching on this side, in painful suspense, to hear how their delegates were received. Judging from my own feelings, the women on both sides of the Atlantic must have been humilated and chagrined, except as these feelings were outweighed by contempt for the shallow reasoning of their opponents and their comical pose and gestures in some of the intensely earnest flights of their imagination.

The clerical portion of the convention was most violent in its opposition. The clergymen seemed to have God and his angels especially in their care and keeping, and were in agony lest the women should do or say something to shock the heavenly hosts. Their all-sustaining conceit gave them abundant assurance that their movements must necessarily be all-pleasing to the celestials whose ears were open to the proceedings of the World's Convention. Deborah, Huldah, Vashti, and Esther might have questioned the propriety of calling it a World's Convention, when only half of humanity was represented there; but what were their opinions worth compared with those of the Rev. A. Harvey, the Rev. C. Stout, or the Rev. J. Burnet, who,

Bible in hand, argued woman's subjection, divinely decreed when Eve was created.

One of our champions in the convention, George Bradburn, a tall thick-set man with a voice like thunder, standing head and shoulders above the clerical representatives, swept all their arguments aside by declaring with tremendous emphasis that, if they could prove to him that the Bible taught the entire subjection of one-half of the race to the other, he should consider that the best thing he could do for humanity would be to bring together every Bible in the universe and make a grand bonfire of them.

It was really pitiful to hear narrow-minded bigots, pretending to be teachers and leaders of men, so cruelly remanding their own mothers, with the rest of womankind, to absolute subjection to the ordinary masculine type of humanity. I always regretted that the women themselves had not taken part in the debate before the convention was fully organized and the question of delegates settled. It seemed to me then, and does now, that all delegates with credentials from recognized societies should have had a voice in the organization of the convention, though subject to exclusion afterward. However, the women sat in a low curtained seat like a church choir, and modestly listened to the French, British, and American Solons for twelve of the longest days in June, as did, also, our grand Garrison and Rogers in the gallery. They scorned a convention that ignored the rights of the very women who had fought, side by side, with them in the anti-slavery conflict. "After battling so many long years," said Garrison, "for the liberties of African slaves, I can take no part in a convention that strikes down the most sacred rights of all women." After coming three thousand miles to speak on the subject nearest his heart, he nobly shared the enforced silence of the rejected delegates. It was a great act of self-sacrifice that should never be forgotten by women.

Thomas Clarkson was chosen president of the convention and made a few remarks in opening, but he soon retired, as his age and many infirmities made all public occasions too burdersome, and Joseph Sturge, a Quaker, was made chairman. Sitting next to Mrs. Mott, I said:

"As there is a Quaker in the chair now, what could he do if the spirit should move you to speak?"

"Ah," she replied, evidently not believing such a contingency possible, "where the spirit of the Lord is, there is liberty."

She had not much faith in the sincerity of abolitionists who, while eloquently defending the natural rights of slaves, denied freedom of speech to one-half the people of their own race. Such was the consistency of an assemblage of philanthropists! They would have been horrified at the idea of burning the flesh of the distinguished women present with red-hot irons, but the crucifixion of their pride and self-respect, the humiliation of the spirit, seemed to them a most trifling matter. The action of this convention was the topic of discussion, in public and private, for a long time, and stung many women into new thought and action and gave rise to the movement for women's political equality both in England and the United States.

As the convention adjourned, the remark was heard on all sides, "It is about time some demand was made for new liberties for women." As Mrs. Mott and I walked home, arm in arm, commenting on the incidents of the day, we resolved to hold a convention as soon as we returned home, and form a society to advocate the rights of women. At the lodging house on Queen Street, where a large number of delegates had apartments, the discussions were heated at every meal, and at times so bitter that, at last, Mr. Birney packed his valise and sought more peaceful quarters. Having strongly opposed the admission of women as delegates to the convention it was rather embarrassing to meet them, during the intervals between the various sessions, at the table and in the drawing room.

These were the first women I had ever met who believed in the equality of the sexes and who did not believe in the popular orthodox religion. The acquaintance of Lucretia Mott, who was a broad, liberal thinker on politics, religion, and all questions of reform, opened to me a new world of thought. As we walked about to see the sights of London, I embraced every opportunity to talk with her. It was intensely gratifying to hear all that, through years of doubt, I had dimly thought, so freely discussed by other women, some of them no older than myself—women, too, of rare intelligence, cultivation, and refinement. . . .

*   *   *

In the spring of 1847 we moved to Seneca Falls. Here we spent sixteen years of our married life, and here our other children—two sons and two daughters—were born.

Just as we were ready to leave Boston, Mr. and Mrs. Eaton and their two children arrived from Europe, and we decided to go together to Johnstown, Mr. Eaton being obliged to hurry to New York on business, and Mr. Stanton to remain still in Boston a few months. At the last moment my nurse decided she could not leave her friends and go so far away. Accordingly my sister and I started, by rail, with five children and seventeen trunks, for Albany, where we rested over night and part of the next day. We had a very fatiguing journey, looking after so many trunks and children, for my sister's children persisted in

Elizabeth Cady Stanton, with two of her children, about the time of the Seneca Falls Convention. *(Courtesy: Library of Congress)*

standing on the platform at every opportunity, and the younger ones would follow their example. This kept us constantly on the watch. We were thankful when safely landed once more in the old homestead in Johnstown, where we arrived at midnight. As our beloved parents had received no warning of our coming, the whole household was aroused to dispose of us. But now in safe harbor, 'mid familiar scenes and pleasant memories, our slumbers were indeed refreshing. How rapidly one throws off all care and anxiety under the parental roof, and how at sea one feels, no matter what the age may be, when the loved ones are gone forever and the home of childhood is but a dream of the past.

After a few days of rest I started, alone, for my new home, quite happy with the responsibility of repairing a house and putting all things in order. I was already acquainted with many of the people and the surroundings in Seneca Falls, as my sister, Mrs. Bayard, had lived there several years, and I had frequently made her long visits. We had quite a magnetic circle of reformers, too, in central New York. At Rochester were William Henry Channing, Frederick Douglass, the Anthonys, Posts, Hallowells, Stebbins,—some grand old Quaker families at Farmington,—the Sedgwicks, Mays, Mills, and Matilda Joslyn Gage at Syracuse; Gerrit Smith at Peterboro, and Beriah Green at Whitesboro.

The house we were to occupy had been closed for some years and needed many repairs, and the grounds, comprising five acres, were overgrown with weeds. My father gave me a check and said, with a smile, "You believe in woman's capacity to do and dare; now go ahead and put your place in order." After a minute survey of the premises and due consultation with one or two sons of Adam, I set the carpenters, painters, paper-hangers, and gardeners at work, built a new kitchen and woodhouse, and in one month took possession. Having left my children with my mother, there were no impediments to a full display of my executive ability. In the purchase of brick, timber, paint, etc., and in making bargains with workmen, I was in frequent consultation with Judge Sackett and Mr. Bascom. The latter was a member of the Constitutional Convention, then in session in Albany, and as he used to walk down whenever he was at home, to see how my work progressed, we had long talks, sitting on boxes in the midst of tools and shavings, on the status of women. I urged him to propose an amendment to Article II, Section 3, of the State Constitution, striking out the word "male," which limits the suffrage to men. But, while he fully agreed with all I had to say on the political equality of women, he had not the courage to make himself the laughing-stock of the convention. Whenever I cornered him on this point, manlike he turned the conversation to the painters and carpenters. However, these conversations had the effect of bringing him into the first woman's convention, where he did us good service.

In Seneca Falls my life was comparatively solitary, and the change from Boston was somewhat depressing. There, all my immediate friends were reformers, I had near neighbors, a new home with all the modern conveniences, and well-trained servants. Here our residence was on the outskirts of the town, roads very often muddy and no sidewalks most of the way, Mr. Stanton was frequently from home, I had poor servants, and an increasing number of children. To keep a house and grounds in good order, purchase every article for daily use, keep the wardrobes of half a dozen human beings in proper trim, take the children to dentists, shoemakers, and different schools, or find teachers at home, altogether made sufficient work to keep one brain busy, as well as all the hands I could impress into the service. Then, too, the novelty of housekeeping had passed away, and much that was once attractive in domestic life was now irksome. I had so many cares that the company I needed for intellectual stimulus was a trial rather than a pleasure.

There was quite an Irish settlement at a short distance, and continual complaints were coming to me that my boys threw stones at their pigs, cows, and the roofs of their houses. This involved constant diplomatic relations in the settlement of various difficulties, in which I was so successful that, at length, they constituted me a kind of umpire in all their own quarrels. If a drunken husband was pounding his wife, the children would run for me. Hastening to the scene of action, I would take Patrick by the collar, and, much to his surprise and shame, make him sit down and promise to behave himself. I never had one of them offer the least resistance, and in time they all came to regard me as one having authority. I strengthened my influence by cultivating good feeling. I lent the men papers to read, and invited their children into our grounds; giving them fruit, of which we had abundance, and my children's old clothes, books, and toys. I was their physician, also—with my box of homeopathic medicines I took charge of the men, women, and children in sickness. Thus the most amicable relations were established, and, in any emergency, these poor neighbors were good friends and always ready to serve me.

But I found police duty rather irksome, especially when called out dark nights to prevent drunken fathers from disturbing their sleeping children, or to minister to poor mothers in the pangs of maternity. Alas! alas! who can measure the mountains of sorrow and suffering endured in unwelcome motherhood in the abodes of ignorance, poverty, and vice, where terror-stricken women and children are the victims of strong men frenzied with passion and intoxicating drink?

Up to this time life had glided by with comparative ease, but now the real struggle was upon me. My duties were too numerous and varied, and none sufficiently exhilarating or intellectual to bring into play my higher faculties. I suffered with mental hunger, which, like an empty stomach, is very depressing. I had books, but no stimulating companionship. To add to my general dissatisfaction at the change from Boston, I found that Seneca Falls was a malarial region, and in due time all the children were attacked with chills and fever which, under homeopathic treatment in those days, lasted three months. The servants were afflicted in the same way. Cleanliness, order, the love of the beautiful and artistic, all faded away in the struggle to accomplish what was absolutely necessary from hour to hour. Now I understood, as I never had before, how women could sit down and rest in the midst of general disorder. Housekeeping, under such conditions, was impossible, so I packed our clothes, locked up the house, and went to that harbor of safety, home, as I did ever after in stress of weather.

I now fully understood the practical difficulties most women had to contend with in the isolated household, and the impossibility of woman's best development if in contact, the chief part of her life, with servants and children. Fourier's phalansterie community life and co-operative households had a new significance for me. Emerson says, "A healthy discontent is the first step to progress." The general discontent I felt with woman's portion as wife, mother, housekeeper, physician, and spiritual guide, the chaotic conditions into which everything fell without her constant supervision, and the wearied, anxious look of the majority of women impressed me with a strong feeling that some active measures should be taken to remedy the wrongs of society in general, and of women in particular. My experience at the World's Anti-slavery Convention, all I had read of the legal status of women, and the oppression I saw everywhere, together swept across my soul, intensified now by many personal experiences. It seemed as if all the elements had conspired to impel me to some onward step. I could not see what to do or where to begin—my only thought was a public meeting for protest and discussion.

In this tempest-tossed condition of mind I received an invitation to spend the day with Lucretia Mott, at Richard Hunt's, in Waterloo. There I met several members of different families of Friends, earnest, thoughtful women. I poured out, that day, the torrent of my long-accumulating discontent, with such vehemence and indignation that I stirred myself, as well as the rest of the party, to do and dare anything. My discontent, according to Emerson, must have been healthy, for it moved us all to prompt action, and we decided, then and there, to call a "Woman's Rights Convention." We wrote the call that evening and published it in the *Seneca County Courier* the next day, the 14th of July, 1848, giving only five days' notice, as the convention was to be held on the 19th and 20th. The call was inserted without signatures,—in fact it was a mere announcement of a meeting,—but the chief movers and managers were Lucretia Mott, Mary Ann McClintock, Jane Hunt, Martha C. Wright, and myself. The convention, which was held two days in the Methodist Church, was in every way a grand success. The house was crowded at every session, the speaking good, and a religious earnestness dignified all the proceedings.

These were the hasty initiative steps of "the most momentous reform that had yet been launched on the world—the first organized protest against the injustice which had brooded for ages over the character and destiny of one-half the race." No words could express our astonishment on finding, a few days afterward, that what seemed to us so timely, so rational, and so sacred, should be a subject for sarcasm and ridicule to the entire press of the nation. With our Declaration of Rights and Resolutions for a text, it seemed as if every man who could wield a pen prepared a homily on "woman's sphere." All the journals from Maine to Texas seemed to strive with each other to see which could make our movement appear the most ridiculous. The anti-slavery papers stood by us manfully and so did Frederick Douglass, both in the convention and in his paper, *The North Star*, but so pronounced was the popular voice against us, in the parlor, press, and pulpit, that most of the ladies who had attended the convention and signed the declaration, one by one, withdrew their names and influence and joined our persecutors. Our friends gave us the cold shoulder and felt themselves disgraced by the whole proceeding.

If I had had the slightest premonition of all that was to follow that convention, I fear I should not have had the courage to risk it, and I must confess that it was with fear and trembling that I consented to attend another, one month afterward, in Rochester. Fortunately, the first one seemed to have drawn all the fire, and of the second but little was said. But we had set the ball in motion, and now, in quick succession, conventions were held in Ohio, Indiana, Massachusetts, Pennsylvania, and in the City of New York, and have been kept up nearly every year since.

Woman's Rights Convention

SENECA COUNTY COURIER, July 14, July 21, August 4, 1848

A small news item on an inside page of the July 14 SENECA COUNTY COURIER marked the beginnings of the women's rights movement in the United States. Because the COURIER was a bi-weekly newspaper, the organizers of the convention were able to have the notice repeated in the July 18 issue—the day before the convention. The day after the meeting ended, the July 21 COURIER carried a straightforward account of the convention and on August 4 printed the resolutions it passed. One of the COURIER's editors was Dexter Chamberlain Bloomer, whose wife, Amelia, was a friend of Elizabeth Cady Stanton.

(July 14)
WOMAN'S RIGHTS CONVENTION.

A Convention to discuss the social, civil and religious condition and rights of Woman, will be held in the Wesleyan Chapel, at Seneca Falls, N.Y., on Wednesday and Thursday the 19th and 20th of July current, commencing at 10 o'clock A.M.

During the first day, the meeting will be exclusively for Women, which all are earnestly invited to attend. The public generally are invited to be present on the second day, when LUCRETIA MOTT, of Philadelphia, and others both ladies and gentlemen, will address the Convention.

*   *   *

Source: Seneca County Courier (14 July; 21 July; 4 Aug. 1848).

(July 21)
WOMAN'S RIGHTS CONVENTION.

This meeting adjourned finally last evening, after a session of two days. The attendance was respectable in numbers and highly respectable in character. The proceedings were of an interesting nature. On the first day, the "lords of creation" were excluded, and we can only speak of the exercises from hearsay. We learn that they consisted chiefly in preparations for the more important business of the convention—the reading and amending of a Declaration of Sentiments—and consulting as to the resolutions which should be proposed. On the evening of the first day, the Wesleyan Chapel, the building in which all the meetings were held—was thrown open to the public, and, at the time appointed for the commencement of business, was filled with an intelligent and respectful audience. The chief speaker was Lucretia Mott, of Philadelphia. This lady is so well known as a pleasing and eloquent orator, that a description of her manner would be a work of supererogation. Her discourse on that evening, whatever may be thought of some of its doctrines, was eminently beautiful and instructive.

James and Lucretia Mott.
(Courtesy: Boston Public Library Photographic Collection)

Her theme was the Progress of Reforms. In illustrating her subject, she described the gradual advancement of the causes of
Temperance, Anti-Slavery, Peace, &c., briefly, but in a neat and
impressive style. She then alluded to the occasion which had
brought the audience together—glanced at the rights and the
wrongs of women—and expressed the hope and belief that the
movement in which she was then participating, would soon
assume a grandeur and dignity worthy of its importance. She
concluded by urging some of the gentlemen to let their voices
be heard on the great subject. This invitation met with no
response, except a brief and humorous apology from Mr. DOUG-
LASS, of the *North Star*. On Thursday, the second day, three
meetings were held. We learn that in the morning, the Declaration of Sentiments was read and adopted. It was then signed
by many persons present. This instrument is constructed after
the plan of the American Declaration of Independence. It is
well drawn and contains a succinct statement of alleged grievances. As far as practicable it adopts the language of its model.
We were present during a part of the afternoon meeting. The
chairman was JAMES MOTT, of Philadelphia—the secretaries,
Miss MARY ANN M'CLINTOCK jr., of Waterloo, and Mrs. STANTON,
of Seneca Falls. Spirited, and spicy resolutions were read, and,
after some remarks from Mrs. MOTT, THOMAS M'CLINTOCK, FRED-
ERICK DOUGLASS, Mrs. STANTON, and GEORGE PRYOR, were passed,
no one expressing dissent. To all persons who disapproved of
the doctrines of the resolutions, repeated opportunities for
reply were offered, but no one responded to them. Mrs. STAN-
TON read an extract from a letter of Wm. HOWITT's, written soon
after the exclusion of the female delegates to the World's Convention of 1840. We have not received any report of the proceedings in the evening.

This convention was novel in its character, and the doctrines broached in it are startling to those who are wedded to
the present usages and laws of society. The resolutions are of
the kind called radical. Some of the speeches were very able—
all the exercises were marked by great order and decorum.
When the Declaration of Sentiments and Resolutions, shall be
printed and circulated, they will provoke much remark. All

will be curious to know their nature. Some will regard them with respect—others with disapprobation and contempt.

*   *   *

(August 4)
RESOLUTIONS PASSED AT THE
WOMAN'S RIGHTS CONVENTION
HELD IN THIS VILLAGE ON THE
19TH AND 20TH INST.

Whereas, the great precept of nature is conceded to be "that man shall pursue his own true and substantial happiness;" Blackstone, in his commentaries, remarks, that this law of Nature being coeval with mankind, and dictated by God himself is, of course, superior in obligation to any other. It is binding over all the globe, in all countries, and at all times: no human laws are of any validity if contrary to this, and such of them as are valid, derive all their force, and all their validity, and all their authority, mediately and immediately from this original.

Therefore, *Resolved*, That such laws as conflict in any way, with the true and substantial happiness of women, are contrary to the great precept of Nature, and of no validity, for this "is superior in obligation to any other."

Resolved, That all laws which prevent woman from occupying such a station in society as her conscience shall dictate, or which place her in a position inferior to that of man, are contrary to the great precept of Nature and therefore of no force or authority.

Resolved, That woman is man's equal, was intended to be so by her Creator, and the highest good of the race demands that she should be recognized as such.

Resolved, That the women of this country ought to be enlightened with regard to the laws under which they live, that they may no longer publish their degradation by declaring themselves satisfied with their present position, nor their ignorance by asserting they have all the rights they want.

Resolved, That inasmuch as man, while claiming for himself intellectual superiority, does accord to woman, moral superiority, it is pre-eminently his duty to encourage her to speak and teach as she has opportunity in all religious assemblies.

Resolved, That the same amount of virtue, delicacy, and refinement of behavior, that is required of woman in the social state, should be required of man, and the same transgressions should be visited with equal severity on both man and woman.

Resolved, That the objection of indelicacy and impropriety which is so often brought against woman when she addresses a public audience, comes with very ill grace from those who encourage by their attendance, her appearance on the stage, in the concert, or in the feats of the circus.

Resolved, That woman has too long rested satisfied in the circumscribed limits which corrupt custom and a perverted application of the Scriptures have marked out for her, and that it is time she should move in the enlarged sphere which her Great Creator has assigned her.

Resolved, That it is the duty of the women of this country to secure to themselves their sacred right to the elective franchise.

Resolved, That the equality of human rights, results necessarily from the fact of the identity of the race in capabilities and responsibilities.

Resolved, Therefore, that being invested by the Creator with the same capabilities, and the same consciousness of responsibility for their exercise, it is demonstrably the right and duty of woman, equally with man, to promote every righteous cause by every righteous means; and especially in regard to the great subjects of morals and religion, it is self-evidently her right to participate with her brother in teaching them, both in private and in public, by writing and by speaking, by any instrumentalities proper to be used, and in any assembly proper to be held; and this being a self-evident truth, growing out of the divinely implanted principles of human nature, any custom or authority adverse to it, whether modern or wearing the hoary sanction of antiquity, is to be regarded as a self-evident falsehood, and at war with the interests of mankind.

Resolved, That the speedy success of our cause depends upon the zealous and untiring efforts of men and women for the overthrow of the monopoly of the pulpit, and for the securing to woman an equal participation with man in the various trades, professions and commerce.

"Declaration of Sentiments," 1848

The following declaration, written in four days, from July 14 to 18, 1848 (the Declaration of Independence, on which it was modeled, had taken Thomas Jefferson and his committee seventeen days, from June 11 to 28, 1776), was officially adopted at the Seneca Falls Convention of July 19–20, 1848. This call for women's equality, audacious for its time, could not fail to attract nationwide attention. But it was too radical on second thought for many affixing their names, who later rescinded their signatures.

When, in the course of human events, it becomes necessary for one portion of the family of man to assume among the people of the earth a position different from that which they have hitherto occupied, but one to which the laws of nature and of nature's God entitle them, a decent respect to the opinions of mankind requires that they should declare the causes that impel them to such a course.

We hold these truths to be self-evident: that all men and women are created equal; that they are endowed by their Creator with certain inalienable rights; that among these are life, liberty, and the pursuit of happiness; that to secure these rights governments are instituted, deriving their just powers from the consent of the governed. Whenever any form of Government becomes destructive of these ends, it is the right of those who

Source: Copy of the Declaration of Sentiments, courtesy of the Seneca Falls Historical Society, Seneca Falls, N.Y.

suffer from it to refuse allegiance to it, and to insist upon the institution of a new government, laying its foundation on such principles, and organizing its powers in such form, as to them shall seem most likely to effect their safety and happiness. Prudence, indeed, will dictate that governments long established should not be changed for light and transient causes; and accordingly all experience hath shown that mankind are more disposed to suffer, while evils are sufferable, than to right themselves by abolishing the forms to which they were accustomed. But when a long train of abuses and usurpations, pursuing invariably the same object evinces a design to reduce them under absolute despotism, it is their duty to throw off such government, and to provide new guards for their future security. Such has been the patient sufferance of the women under this government, and such is now the necessity which constrains them to demand the equal station to which they are entitled.

The history of mankind is a history of repeated injuries and usurpations on the part of man toward woman, having in direct object the establishment of an absolute tyranny over her. To prove this, let facts be submitted to a candid world.

He has never permitted her to exercise her inalienable right to the elective franchise.

He has compelled her to submit to laws, in the formation of which she had no voice.

He has withheld from her rights which are given to the most ignorant and degraded men—both natives and foreigners.

Having deprived her of this first right of a citizen, the elective franchise, thereby leaving her without representation in the halls of legislation, he has oppressed her on all sides.

He has made her, if married, in the eye of the law, civilly dead.

He has taken from her all right in property, even to the wages she earns.

He has made her, morally, an irresponsible being, as she can commit many crimes with impunity, provided they be done in the presence of her husband. In the covenant of marriage, she is compelled to promise obedience to her husband, he becoming to all intents and purposes, her master—the law giving him power to deprive her of her liberty, and to administer chastisement.

He has so framed the laws of divorce, as to what shall be the proper causes of divorce, and in case of separation, to whom the guardianship of the children shall be given, as to be wholly regardless of the happiness of women—the law, in all cases, going upon a false supposition of the supremacy of man, and giving all power into his hands.

After depriving her of all rights as a married woman, if single and the owner of property, he has taxed her to support a government which recognizes her only when her property can be made profitable to it.

He has monopolized nearly all the profitable employments, and from those she is permitted to follow, she receives but a scanty remuneration.

He closes against her all the avenues to wealth and distinction, which he considers most honorable to himself. As a teacher of theology, medicine, or law, she is not known.

He has denied her the facilities for obtaining a thorough education—all colleges being closed against her.

He allows her in Church as well as State, but a subordinate position, claiming Apostolic authority for her exclusion from the ministry, and, with some exceptions, from any public participation in the affairs of the Church.

He has created a false public sentiment by giving to the world a different code of morals for men and women, by which moral delinquencies which exclude women from society, are not only tolerated, but deemed of little account in man.

He has usurped the prerogative of Jehovah himself, claiming it as his right to assign for her a sphere of action, when that belongs to her conscience and to her God.

He has endeavored, in every way that he could, to destroy her confidence in her own powers, to lessen her self-respect, and to make her willing to lead a dependent and abject life.

Now, in view of this entire disfranchisement of one-half the people of this country, their social and religious degradation,—

in view of the unjust laws above mentioned, and because women do feel themselves aggrieved, oppressed, and fraudulently deprived of their most sacred rights, we insist that they have immediate admission to all the rights and privileges which belong to them as citizens of these United States.

In entering upon the great work before us, we anticipate no small amount of misconception, misrepresentation, and ridicule; but we shall use every instrumentality within our power to effect our object. We shall employ agents, circulate tracts, petition the State and national Legislatures, and endeavor to enlist the pulpit and the press in our behalf. We hope this Convention will be followed by a series of Conventions, embracing every part of the country.

Firmly relying upon the final triumph of the Right and the True, we do this day affix our signatures to this declaration.

SIGNERS OF THE DECLARATION OF SENTIMENTS
SENECA FALLS • NEW YORK • JULY 19–20 • 1848

Barker, Caroline	Hoffman, Sarah
Barker, Eunice	Hoskins, Charles L.
Barker, William G.	Hunt, Jane C.
Bonnel, Rachel D. (Mitchell)	Hunt, Richard P.
Bunker, Joel D.	Jenkins, Margaret
Burroughs, William	Jones, John
Capron, E. W.	Jones, Lucy
Chamberlain, Jacob P.	King, Phebe
Conklin, Elizabeth	Latham, Hannah J.
Conklin, Mary	Latham, Lovina
Culvert, P.A.	Leslie, Elizabeth
Davis, Cynthia	Martin, Eliza
Dell, Thomas	Martin, Mary
Dell, William S.	Mathews, Delia
Doty, Elias J.	Mathews, Dorothy
Doty, Susan R.	Mathews, Jacob
Douglass, Frederick	M'Clintock, Elizabeth W.
Drake, Julia Ann	M'Clintock, Mary
Eaton, Harriet Cady	M'Clintock, Mary Ann
Foote, Elisha	M'Clintock, Thomas
Foote, Eunice Newton	Metcalf, Jonathan
Frink, Mary Ann	Milliken, Nathan J.
Fuller, Cynthia	Mirror, Mary S.
Gibbs, Experience	Mosher, Pheobe
Gilbert, Mary	Mosher, Sarah A.
Gild, Lydia	Mott, James
Hallowell, Sarah	Mott, Lucretia
Hallowell, Mary H.	Mount, Lydia
Hatley, Henry	Paine, Catharine C.

Palmer, Rhoda
Phillips, Saron
Pitcher, Sally
Plant, Hannah
Porter, Ann
Post, Amy
Pryor, George W.
Pryor, Margaret
Quinn, Susan
Race, Rebecca
Ridley, Martha
Schooley, Azaliah
Schooley, Margaret
Scott, Deborah
Segur, Antoinette E.
Seymour, Henry
Seymour, Henry W.
Seymour, Malvina
Shaw, Catharine
Shear, Stephen
Sisson, Sarah

Smallbridge, Robert
Smith, Elizabeth D.
Smith, Sarah
Spalding, David
Spalding, Lucy
Stanton, Elizabeth Cady
Stebbins, Catharine F.
Taylor, Sophronia
Tewksbury, Betsey
Tillman, Samuel D.
Underhill, Edward F.
Underhill, Martha
Vail, Mary E.
Van Tassel, Isaac
Whitney, Sarah
Wilbur, Maria E.
Williams, Justin
Woods, Sarah R.
Woodward, Charlotte
Woodworth, S.E.
Wright, Martha C.

The Proceedings

REPORT.

A CONVENTION to discuss the SOCIAL, CIVIL, AND RELIGIOUS CONDITION OF WOMAN, was called by the Women of Seneca County, N. Y., and held at the village of Seneca Falls, in the Wesleyan Chapel, on the 19th and 20th of July, 1848.

The question was discussed throughout two entire days: the first day by women exclusively, the second day men participated in the deliberations. LUCRETIA MOTT, of Philadelphia, was the moving spirit of the occasion.

On the morning of the 19th, the Convention assembled at 11 o'clock. The meeting was organized by appointing MARY M'CLINTOCK Secretary. The object of the meeting was then stated by ELIZABETH C. STANTON; after which, remarks were made by LUCRETIA MOTT, urging the women present to throw aside the trammels of education, and not allow their new position to prevent them from joining in the debates of the meeting. The Declaration of Sentiments, offered for the acceptance of the Convention, was then read by E. C. STANTON. A proposition was made to have it re-read by paragraph, and after much consideration, some changes were suggested and adopted. The propriety of obtaining the signatures of men to the Declaration was discussed in an animated manner: a vote in favor was given; but concluding that the final decision would be the legitimate business of the next day, it was referred.

Adjourned to half-past two.

In the afternoon, the meeting assembled according to adjournment, and was opened by reading the minutes of the morning session. E. C. STANTON then addressed the meeting,

Source: Seneca Falls Historical Society, Seneca Falls, N.Y.

and was followed by LUCRETIA MOTT. The reading of the Declaration was called for, an addition having been inserted since the morning session. A vote taken upon the amendment was carried, and papers circulated to obtain signatures. The following resolutions were then read: . . . [*See the resolutions as printed in the* Seneca County Courier, *August 4, pp. 82–84.*]

LUCRETIA MOTT read a humorous article from a newspaper, written by MARTHA C. WRIGHT. After an address by E. W. M'CLINTOCK, the meeting adjourned to 10 o'clock the next morning.

In the evening, LUCRETIA MOTT spoke with her usual eloquence and power to a large and intelligent audience on the subject of Reforms in general.

THURSDAY MORNING.

The Convention assembled at the hour appointed, JAMES MOTT, of Philadelphia, in the Chair. The minutes of the previous day having been read, E. C. STANTON again read the Declaration of Sentiments, which was freely discussed by LUCRETIA MOTT, ANSEL BASCOM, S. E. WOODWORTH, THOMAS and MARY ANN M'CLINTOCK, FREDERICK DOUGLASS, AMY POST, CATHARINE STEBBINS, and ELIZABETH C. STANTON, and was unanimously adopted. . . .

The meeting adjourned until two o'clock.

AFTERNOON SESSION.

At the appointed hour the meeting convened. The minutes having been read, the resolutions of the day before were read and taken up separately. Some, from their self-evident truth, elicited but little remark; others, after some criticism, much debate, and some slight alterations, were finally passed by a large majority. The meeting closed with a forcible speech from LUCRETIA MOTT.

Adjourned to half-past seven o'clock.

EVENING SESSION.

The meeting opened by reading the minutes, THOMAS M'CLINTOCK in the Chair. As there had been no opposition expressed during the Convention to this movement, and although, after repeated invitation, no objections had presented themselves, E. C. STANTON volunteered an address in defence of the many severe accusations brought against the much-abused "Lords of Creation."

THOMAS M'CLINTOCK then read several extracts from Blackstone, in proof of woman's servitude to man; after which LUCRETIA MOTT offered and spoke to the following resolution:

Resolved, That the speedy success of our cause depends upon the zealous and untiring efforts of both men and women, for the overthrow of the monopoly of the pulpit, and for the securing to woman an equal participation with men in the various trades, professions and commerce.

The Resolution was adopted.

M. A. M'CLINTOCK, Jr. delivered a short, but impressive address, calling upon woman to arouse from her lethargy and be true to herself and her God. When she had concluded, FREDERICK DOUGLASS arose, and in an excellent and appropriate speech, ably supported the cause of woman.

The meeting was closed by one of LUCRETIA MOTT's most beautiful and spiritual appeals. She commanded the earnest attention of that large audience for nearly an hour.

M. A. M'CLINTOCK, E. N. FOOTE, AMY POST, E. W. M'CLINTOCK, and E. C. STANTON, were appointed a Committee to prepare the proceedings of the Convention for publication.

"The Rights of Women"

THE NORTH STAR, July 28, 1848

Frederick Douglass was a signer of the Seneca Falls Declaration of Sentiments and a staunch supporter of women's rights, as this selection from THE NORTH STAR proves. "The Rights of Women" appeared just eight days after the first women's rights convention. Another convention was held barely two weeks later, in Rochester, New York. Other meetings would soon follow, in states from Ohio to Massachusetts—but none in the southern states. There northern newspapers did not circulate, and the women's rights cause was perceived as too closely tied to the antislavery movement. Southern women, if they thought about women's rights, did so in private.

One of the most interesting events of the past week, was the holding of what is technically styled a Woman's Rights Convention, at Seneca Falls. The speaking, addresses, and resolutions of this extraordinary meeting, were almost wholly conducted by women; and although they evidently felt themselves in a novel position, it is but simple justice to say, that their whole proceedings were characterized by marked ability and dignity. No one present, we think, however much he might be disposed to differ from the views advanced by the leading speakers on that occasion, will fail to give them credit for brilliant talents and excellent dispositions. In this meeting, as in other deliberative assemblies, there were frequently differences

Source: "The Rights of Women," *The North Star* 1, no. 31 (28 July 1848).

of opinion and animated discussion; but in no case was there the slightest absence of good feeling and decorum. Several interesting documents, setting forth the rights as well as the grievances of woman, were read. Among these was a declaration of sentiments, to be regarded as the basis of a grand movement for attaining all the civil, social, political and religious rights of woman. As these documents are soon to be published in pamphlet form, under the authority of a Committee of women, appointed by that meeting, we will not mar them by attempting any synopsis of their contents. We should not, however, do justice to our own convictions or to the excellent persons connected with this infant movement, if we did not, in this connection, offer a few remarks on the general subject which the Convention met to consider, and the objects they seek to attain.

In doing so, we are not insensible that the bare mention of this truly important subject in any other than terms of contemptuous ridicule and scornful disfavor, is likely to excite against us the fury of bigotry and the folly of prejudice. A discussion of the rights of animals would be regarded with far more complacency by many of what are called the *wise* and the *good* of our land, than would be a discussion of the rights of woman. It is, in their estimation, to be guilty of evil thoughts, to think that woman is entitled to rights equal with man. Many who have at last made the discovery that negroes have some rights as well as other members of the human family, have yet to be convinced that woman is entitled to any. Eight years ago, a number of persons of this description actually abandoned the anti-slavery cause, lest by giving their influence in that direction, they might possibly be giving countenance to the dangerous heresy that woman, in respect to rights, stands on an equal footing with man. In the judgment of such persons, the American slave system, with all its concomitant horrors, is less to be deplored than this *wicked* idea. It is perhaps needless to say, that we cherish little sympathy for such sentiments, or respect for such prejudices. Standing as we do upon the watch-tower of human freedom, we cannot be deterred from an expression of our approbation of any movement; however humble, to improve and elevate the character and condition of any members of the human family. While it is impossible for us to go into this subject at length, and dispose of the various objections which are often urged against such a doctrine as that of female equality, we are free to say, that in respect to political rights, we hold woman to be justly entitled to all we claim for man. We go farther, and express our conviction that all political rights which it is expedient for man to exercise, it is equally so for woman. All that distinguishes man as an intelligent and accountable being, is equally true of woman; and if that government is only just which governs by the free consent of the governed, there can be no reason in the world for denying to woman the exercise of the elective franchise, or a hand in making and administering the laws of the land. Our doctrine is, that "Right is of no sex." We therefore bid the women engaged in this movement our humble God speed.

Views of "Woman's Sphere"

In the summer of 1848 a young medical student named Elizabeth Blackwell heard of the women's rights meeting at Seneca Falls. She had already set out on her own feminist journey by being accepted for study at the Geneva Medical College in upstate New York, and she would soon become the first woman in the United States or Europe ever to graduate from a medical school. In 1851 she would begin her medical practice in New York City, and later helped to found the New York Infirmary for Women and Children. In August of 1848 she wrote the following letter to Emily Collins, one of the early women's rights workers in New York. In it she set down her views on the condition of women and her hopes for the "true ennoblement of woman."

LETTER OF ELIZABETH BLACKWELL, 1848

PHILADELPHIA, *August* 12, 1848.

DEAR MADAM:—Your letter, I can assure you, met with a hearty welcome from me. And I can not refrain from writing to you a warm acknowledgment of your cordial sympathy, and expressing the pleasure with which I have read your brave words. It is true, I look neither for praise nor blame in pursuing the path which I have chosen. With firm religious enthusiasm,

Source: Elizabeth Cady Stanton, Susan B. Anthony et al., *The History of Woman Suffrage* (6 vols.; New York, 1881–1922; reprint, New York, 1969), vol. 1.

Elizabeth Blackwell, in later years. *(Courtesy: Schlesinger Library, Radcliffe College)*

no opinion of the world will move me, but when I receive from a woman an approval so true-hearted and glowing, a recognition so clear of the motives which urge me on, then my very soul bounds at the thrilling words, and I go on with renewed energy, with hope, and holy joy in my inmost being.

My whole life is devoted unreservedly to the service of my sex. The study and practice of medicine is in my thought but one means to a great end, for which my very soul yearns with intensest passionate emotion, of which I have dreamed day and night, from my earliest childhood, for which I would offer up my life with triumphant thanksgiving, if martyrdom could secure that glorious end:—the true ennoblement of woman, the full harmonious development of her unknown nature, and the consequent redemption of the whole human race. "Earth waits for her queen." Every noble movement of the age, every prophecy of future glroy, every throb of that great heart which is laboring throughout Christendom, call on woman with a voice of thunder, with the authority of a God, to listen to the mighty summons to awake from her guilty sleep, and rouse to glorious action to play her part in the great drama of the ages, and finish the work that man has begun.

Most fully do I respond to all the noble aspirations that fill your letter. Women are feeble, narrow, frivolous at present: ignorant of their own capacities, and undeveloped in thought and feeling; and while they remain so, the great work of human regeneration must remain incomplete; humanity will continue to suffer, and cry in vain for deliverance, for woman has her work to do, and no one can accomplish it for her. She is bound to rise, to try her strength, to break her bonds;—not with noisy outcry, not with fighting or complaint; but with quiet strength, with gentle dignity, firmly, irresistibly, with a cool determination that never wavers, with a clear insight into her own capacities, let her do her duty, pursue her highest conviction of right, and firmly grasp whatever she is able to carry.

Much is said of the oppression woman suffers; man is reproached with being unjust, tyrannical, jealous. I do not so read human life. The exclusion and constraint woman suffers, is not the result of purposed injury or premeditated insult. It has arisen naturally, without violence, simply because woman has desired nothing more, has not felt the soul too large for the body. But when woman, with matured strength, with steady purpose, presents her lofty claim, all barriers will give way, and man will welcome, with a thrill of joy, the new birth of his sister spirit, the advent of his partner, his co-worker, in the great universe of being.

If the present arrangements of society will not admit of woman's free development, then society must be remodeled, and adapted to the great wants of all humanity. Our race is one, the interests of all are inseparably united, and harmonic freedom for the perfect growth of every human soul is the great want of our time. It has given me heartfelt satisfaction, dear madam, that you sympathize in my effort to advance the great interests of humanity. I feel the responsibility of my position, and I shall endeavor, by wisdom of action, purity of motive, and unwavering steadiness of purpose, to justify the noble hope I have excited. To me the future is full of glorious promise, humanity is arousing to accomplish its grand destiny, and in the fellowship of this great hope, I would greet you, and recognize in your noble spirit a fellow-laborer for the true and the good.

ELIZABETH BLACKWELL.

*   *   *

In October 1848 as the effects of the Seneca Falls convention continued to ripple throughout the Northeast and the Midwest, Emily Collins, an organizer of a women's rights group in South Bristol, New York, wrote to a fellow feminist at Rochester describing the founding of the Women's Equal Rights Union in her small rural community, and proposing a course of action.

LETTER OF WOMEN'S RIGHTS ORGANIZER EMILY COLLINS, 1848

I should have acknowledged the receipt of yours of the 1st inst. earlier, but wished to report somewhat of progress whenever I should write. Our prospects here are brightening. Every lady of any worth or intelligence adopts unhesitatingly our view, and concurs in our measures. On the 19th inst. we met and organized a Woman's Equal Rights Union. Living in the country, where the population is sparse, we are consequently few; but hope to make up in zeal and energy for our lack of numbers. We breathe a freer, if not a purer atmosphere here among the mountains, than do the dwellers in cities,—have more independence,—are less subject to the despotism of fashion, and are less absorbed with dress and amusements. . . . A press entirely devoted to our cause seems indispensable. If there is none such, can you tell me of any paper that advocates our claims more warmly than the *North Star!* A lecturer in the field would be most desirable; but how to raise funds to sustain one is the question. I never really wished for Aladdin's lamp till

Source: Elizabeth Cady Stanton, Susan B. Anthony et al., *The History of Woman Suffrage* (6 vols.; New York, 1881–1922; reprint, New York, 1969), vol. 1.

now. Would to Heaven that women could be persuaded to use the funds they acquire by their sewing-circles and fairs, in trying to raise their own condition above that of "infants, idiots, and lunatics," with whom our statutes class them, instead of spending the money in decorating their churches, or sustaining a clergy, the most of whom are striving to rivet the chains still closer that bind, not only our own sex, but the oppressed of every class and color.

The elective franchise is now the one object for which we must labor; that once attained, all the rest will be easily acquired. Moral Reform and Temperance Societies may be multiplied *ad infinitum*, but they have about the same effect upon the evils they seek to cure, as clipping the top of a hedge would have toward extirpating it. Please forward me a copy of the petition for suffrage. We will engage to do all we can, not only in our own town, but in the adjoining ones of Richmond, East Bloomfield, Canandaigua, and Naples. I have promises of aid from people of influence in obtaining signatures. In the meantime we wish to disseminate some able work upon the enfranchisement of women. We wish to present our Assembly-man elect, whoever he may be, with some work of this kind, and solicit his candid attention to the subject. People are more willing to be convinced by the calm perusal of an argument, than in a personal discussion.

THE FLOWERING OF THE WOMEN'S MOVEMENT: *THE LILY* (1849–1856)

The Lily (1849–1856)

Amelia Bloomer's newspaper, THE LILY, begun as a temperance journal in 1849, soon became the voice of the women's rights movement in the early 1850s, with many of its articles written by Elizabeth Cady Stanton. Bloomer, a resident of Seneca Falls, became famous in the early 1850s for her advocacy of a new mode of women's dress with loose, billowing trousers replacing the cumbersome petticoats and skirts that most mid-nineteenth-century women wore. She did not invent the costume (Libby Smith Miller, a cousin of Elizabeth Cady Stanton and the daughter of abolitionist Gerrit Smith, did that), but in 1852 THE LILY printed a sketch of the outfit, which became known as the "Bloomer costume." THE LILY ceased publication in 1856, when Amelia Bloomer sold the paper after she and her husband moved to Council Bluffs, Iowa.

"Woman's Work in the Temperance Cause"

THE LILY, March 1, 1849

That woman has reason to feel deeply on the subject of Intemperance all must admit. It strikes directly at her happiness, and peace of mind. If she keep herself unpolluted from the touch of the foul destroyer, still its evils assail her not the less surely, or the less fatally. Deep are the feelings of love, and affection, implanted in her breast, and how often, and how cruelly, are these lacerated and rendered the source of intense misery, by witnessing the terrible consequences which flow from the use of intoxicating drinks! How often is her heart made to bleed over the ruin of her fondest hopes! She sees those whom she loves more than life itself, ruined in body and soul—their peace destroyed—their hopes blasted, and their bodies consigned to a drunkard's grave. Upon her too, these evils fall even more directly.—Poverty and wretchedness—a broken heart and a desolate house—beggared offspring and a ruined character—these, all these are the bequests Intemperance makes to woman!

And can she—shall she sit idle, and permit this terrible evil thus to inflict upon her its cruel visitings, and do nothing to stay its progress? No! she cannot—she should not. She is called upon as she loves her own peace of mind—as she loves the happiness of these with whom she is connected in life, to come forth and do what she may to banish the evils of intemperance from the land.—We have long felt this to be her duty. We have

Source: "Woman's Work in the Temperance Cause," *The Lily* 1, no. 3 (1 Mar. 1849).

long felt that woman was called upon to act, and act efficiently in the work of advancing the great temperance cause. Indeed, we think there are few who will deny, that woman has a work to do in this matter. But how is that work to be done? How shall she act in such a manner as to produce the much desired result of banishing entirely the use of strong drink from society?

We propose briefly to answer this enquiry, and show some of the modes by which woman can promote the temperance cause.

She must adhere strictly to the rules of total abstinence herself. This is the starting point.—No one can do any thing effectually in promoting temperance unless their own life corresponds with their professions. And she should make manifest her principles of total abstinence by affixing her name to the Pledge—as then her example will be more likely to be known and followed. She may do much—very much, by instilling into the minds of her children the principles of temperance. From the time their tender minds are capable of comprehending the lessons taught, it should be her study, by depicting to them the horrors of intemperance, to imprint upon their hearts a perfect hatred of all that can intoxicate, and a love of the principles of temperance. She should adopt as her own the language of the poet, and say

> "Oh! if there is one law above the rest,
> Written in wisdom,—if there is a word
> That I would trace as with a pen of fire
> Upon the unwrit tablet of a child,
> Tis *temperance*,—tis abstinence entire
> From alcoholic poison."

She must at all times, and in all places, give her influence in favor of total abstinence. To furnish intoxicating drinks as an article of entertainment to others, is an act unbecoming and unworthy of a friend of temperance. We should banish the destroyer from our dwellings, and should use our influence in all possible ways to induce others to do likewise. A word, or a

"Signing the Pledge." A temperance society lithograph of 1846.
(Courtesy: Library of Congress)

look from woman, may, and has had an influence to save many from a drunkard's grave.

She should give her countenance to all proper and honest efforts to advance the temperance cause. This she can do by attending temperance meetings, and thus by her presence and approval, excite others to action; and by reading, and disseminating sound temperance literature throughout the community, and assisting others in doing a similar work.

She should strive to alleviate the sorrows of those who are suffering from the evils of intemperance. Often then will she have the power to lead its victims back to the paths of sobriety and virtue, and to bind up the wounds of the afflicted, and broken hearted. This surely is a work which woman can best perform, and in it most certainly succeed.

She ought to discountenance in all proper ways the unholy traffic in intoxicating liquors. The pledge adopted by the

Ladies' Society of this village contains this principle, and is, we think, well worthy of approval. We are satisfied that the friends of temperance must, if they would act consistently, take this stand, and maintain it, and it becomes our sex to do their part in carrying out this principle. And in this connection we would add, that to associate with, or to permit those to become our associates, who are in the habit of using strong drink, is in a high degree unworthy (where such associates can be avoided) of the professed friends of temperance. If we would refuse all such associations, and cultivate only the society of the virtuous and good, then should we show forth to the world that our practice does not belie our profession.

Finally—we recommend the formation of Female Temperance societies. We believe they may be the means of doing much good. With us, as with men, more may be done by combined effort than singly; and we can thus make our influence more surely felt. We believe such associations may be conducted in a manner becoming the retiring modesty of our sex—without noise or parade, and in accordance with the strictest rules of propriety.

"The influence we exert in community is not like the noisy bubbling brooklet, whose source is merely the pool formed by the summer shower; but like the quiet course of a deeper stream,

Which ever hath a peaceful, silent flow."

We have thus sketched some of the ways in which woman can work in the temperance cause. We commend these thoughts to the consideration of our readers, and especially to those of our own sex. We hope that from them they may gather some hints to guide them in their labors, if not arouse one, and all, to generous and unceasing labor, in the great work of Temperance Reform.

"Temperance and Politics"

THE LILY, September 1, 1849

We hear a great cry from some quarters about bringing the temperance question into politics, and some try to make themselves and others believe that the advocates of temperance are trying to make political capital out of that question. For one we believe that the temperance question should be made a political one, so far as to obtain good rulers, who will make a prohibitory law against the sale of intoxicating drinks as a beverage, and inflicting a heavy penalty of fine and imprisonment against those who should violate such law. Nay, we believe it to be the duty of the voters of this country who wish for the prosperity and happiness of their fellow-men—who wish to see their country maintain its freedom and independence—and who would see their children grow up wise and virtuous citizens of an enlightened land, instead of becoming a besotted and degraded people—to so cast their ballots that they shall tell against the evil with which we are now inflicted. It is not the true friends of temperance who fear to have this question made a political one; the cry is raised by the vender of the poison and his minions, who fear to have any action taken on the subject, knowing but too well the consequences which will result to them should the cause finally triumph.

But we see no reason why any one need sacrifice his politics in this matter. Let it be seen that temperance men are sincere and in earnest on the subject, and determined to carry out

Source: "Temperance and Politics," *The Lily* 1, no. 9 (1 Sept. 1849).

107

their principles at the polls, and each party will soon find it to be for its interest to nominate such men for office as are worthy of the suffrages of the people. We have too long sent drunkards to our legislature to make our laws, and it is time that they were shown that the people will not always be trifled with.

If either party refuses to support men for office who are strictly opposed to licensing the sale of intoxicating drinks, then its candidates should never receive the support of consistent temperance men. We believe that ere many more election days shall pass, politicians will find themselves compelled by the force of public sentiment to turn their attention to this matter in earnest.

We ladies have no voice in choosing our rulers, and are denied the privilege of making known our wishes, and claiming our rights at the hands of government; it is therefore the more necessary that we exert our powers of persuasion; and use our influence with our fathers, husbands and brothers, to induce them to take a decided stand against the farther encroachments of the tyrant which has invaded many households, and made desolate many happy homes; and also to spare no effort to drive it from existence. We believe that if our sex could have a realizing sense of the vast amount of good they might do, and of the untold happiness which would result from their labors, to thousands of miserable men, women and children, they would not remain so careless and unconcerned in regard to this great and important subject. We have frequently heard gentlemen say that the ladies possessed moral power sufficient if they would but exert it, to banish intemperance entirely from our land in one year. We believe this to be true.

Shall we then fold our hands and sit at ease, when there is such a work for us to do? Shall we trifle and fritter away our time when the moral renovation of a world is calling us to action? Shall we see our children corrupted, and offered as sacrifices to glut the thirsty tyrant, and make no effort to save them, when we can do so, if we will? Arouse, sisters to your duty! Gird on the garment of love to your fellow creatures and form the high resolve to crush the enemy which is stabbing them to the heart. If we may not go ourselves to the polls, let us give the men over whom we have an influence no peace, until they consent to make our votes their own, and deposit them for us. We have a right to demand this of them. We have a right to *demand* at the hands of our rulers, protection against this cruel oppressor, and we should not cease our cry until they are made to listen and heed it.

INCREASE OF INTEMPERANCE.

It is painful for us to witness the increase of intemperance in our village. Scarcely a day passes but we see some one intoxicated in our streets. The rum shops seem to stand open day and night, and on the sabbath especially, the sale of alcohol seems to increase tenfold, and men and boys are sent out from them to disgrace our village and fill our ears with their blasphemous ravings. We are shocked at these enormities. They are standing libels upon all our professions of morality and religion. Our constables and justices find plenty of business in sending these victims of the rumseller to jail, and they will run up long and large bills which the people will some day be called upon to pay.

It makes our blood run cold and causes us to blush for our citizens when we see these poor misguided wretches who have been destroyed through their agency, led as victims to the slaughter, while the fiends who have worked their ruin stand carelessly by and join in the laugh and the sneer excited by the ravings of their maddened victims. We have witnessed several such scenes of late where we counted some three or four of our rumsellers standing in the crowd which had gathered round some poor creature whom they had stripped and ruined; and we have felt a wish that we might be allowed to deal justice to both them and their victims. We would endeavor to raise up the fallen ones and restore them to the happiness and comfort they had lost—or rather which had been wrested from them; while we would deal out to their destroyers punishment according to their deeds. . . .

"Woman's Rights"

THE LILY, October 1, 1849

Fear not dear reader, as your eye rests upon the above words, nor think that we are going to nominate either you or ourself for the Governorship or the Presidency. No, it is not time to make lady Presidents yet, and for ourself we can say that we have no aspirations of the kind at present;—but according to the belief of some, the day will soon come when woman may claim her "rights," in this respect, and then we may not be backward in taking a seat in the Presidential chair, provided the good people shall so will it.

It is not our right to hold office or to rule our country, that we would now advocate. Much, very much, must be done to elevate and improve the character and minds of our sex, before we are capable of ruling our own households as we ought, to say nothing of holding in our hands the reins of government. But woman has rights which she knows not of, or knowing, disregards. She has rights of which she is deprived—or rather, of which she deprives herself. She is willing to sit down within the narrow sphere assigned her by man, and make no effort to obtain her just rights, or free herself from the oppressions which are crushing her to the earth. She tamely submits to be governed by such laws as man sees fit to make, and in making which she has no voice. We know that many of us think we have rights enough, and we are content with what we have; but we forget how many thousand wives and mothers worthy as ourselves, are compelled by the unjust laws of our land, to drag out a weary life and submit to indignities which no man would

---

Source: "Woman's Rights," *The Lily* 1, no. 10 (1 Oct. 1849).

bear. It is stated that thirty thousand die annually from the effects of intoxicating drinks; an equal number of drunkards must stand ready to fall. Think of the wives and mothers of this great number—of their untold griefs—of their hidden sorrows—of their broken hearts—of their hunger and nakedness—their unwearied toil to procure a bare pittance to save their little ones from starvation—of the wretched life they lead, and the unmourned death they die. Think of all this, and then tell us not that woman has her rights. Many of the number thus destroyed inch by inch, have been reared amid all the luxuries that wealth and power can bestow. Many of them possess accomplishments that might have graced the most refined society, and who, had their lots been differently cast, would have been courted and sought after by those who now spurn them—and for what? Simply because they have been so unfortunate as to wed a drunkard—or rather because they upon whom they bestowed their young affections, and who vowed to love and protect them, have proved false to all their vows, and left them to the rough blasts of an unpitying world. What rights have the drunkards wife and children?—Who listens to their tale of woe, or lends a pitying ear to their cry?

A woman is entitled to the same rights as man, but does she have them? Dare men pretend that she does? What right have they to make laws which deprive her of every comfort, strips her of every friend, and dooms her to a wretched existence? And yet they do this, and then if she dare to complain, and ask to be relieved from these tyrannical laws, she is thought to be out of her place, and overstepping the bounds of female delicacy! This is why they so tamely submit to martyrdom by the laws. The statute book of this free country bears upon its leaves a foul stain called a license law. By this law men are bidden to go forth and pursue a business which deprives thirty thousand annually of life—worse than murders of twenty thousand wives and mothers, and sixty thousand children. For the privilege thus allowed, the law claims in return a few dollars from those who pursue this *moral* and *honorable* business! It is useless for our sex to seek redress at the hands of the law, from the cruel wrongs inflicted upon them, for it will give them none—it does not recognise their right to protection. But should they dare to raise their hand against their destroyers, and return injury for injury, then the law quickly defends its agents and metes out punishment for her who ventures to defend herself.

We ask not for the honors or emoluments of office for our sex, but we claim that they are unjustly deprived of their rights. We do not believe that man has the *right*, if he has the power, to make laws which will deprive us of any of the comforts of life—or if he does make such laws without our consent, we are not bound to obey them. Unless those who claim the power of legislating for us, will do something to ameliorate the condition of the downtrodden victims of their cruel enactments, it is not only the right, but the duty of those trampled upon, to assert their claim to protection.

*   *   *

HOME EFFORT.

There is too much reason to deprecate the lack of home effort, to promote the cause of temperance at the present time. Apart from the regular meeting of the Sons of Temperance, we seldom have a local temperance meeting, or hear of the doings of a local temperance society. The neighborhood and village meetings—the assembling together in school houses, public halls and churches, to talk over, discuss and devise means to rid our country of its direct foe, so common a few years since, are now almost entirely unknown. Too much reliance is placed upon lecturers from abroad. Temperance meetings can now it would seem, only be held when an agent of the State Society, or some noted advocate of temperance makes his appearance. Then an effort is made to get up a meeting—then money is advanced to pay the expenses both of the meeting and the speaker; a temporary excitement is enkindled—a fine speech is perhaps listened to, and then the subject is forgotten. No effort is made to follow up the good that has been done; the feeling is suffered to die out, and ere another speaker comes along the state of the cause is as bad or worse than before.

Now we think all this is wrong. There should be more effort made at home, and in the good old Washingtonian style. Every town, village and country must depend mainly upon its own exertions, to root out and break down the evil.—Public lecturers from abroad are well enough in their place, but they cannot do all the work.—Their meetings when properly attended, anwer a good purpose; they arouse public attention, and obtain an audience from many who could not otherwise be reached. But their labors and their meetings must be preceded and followed by the united and devoted effort of every friend of the cause. Men should array themselves on the side of sobriety, not once in a year or once in six months, but every month—aye, every day. The enemy is constantly at work. His recruiting houses with agents, whose business it is to induce men by false pretences, to enlist in the army of the tyrant king, stand constantly open. His flag is never struck—his watch never abandoned, but with ceaseless application he plys the arts and devices of his vocation, to lead immortal souls to irretrievable ruin. The soldiers of the temperance army should be equally vigilant. They should fight in divisions, by regiments, in companies, by platoons, and if need be, singly. Not alone when the Major General is on the field must the true soldier show himself a warrior, but equally valiantly must he fight in the presence of his captain or his sergeant, and if need be, he must acquit himself right manfully when attacked alone and in single combat.

Our plea then is for more home effort, more village and town meetings—more zeal in spreading the principles of temperance in our daily walk, and among our daily associates. No town should be without a well organized temperance society. No month, or if possible, no week, should be allowed to pass without the holding of a temperance meeting. When the public lecturer comes along, give him a warm reception—give him a large audience, but when he is gone, think not all the work is accomplished, but follow it up with continued and unceasing effort.

"Woman's Rights"

THE LILY, April 1850

Some of our gentlemen readers are a little troubled lest we should injure ourself and our paper by saying too much in behalf of the rights and interests of our own sex, and it has even been intimated to us that we are controlled in the matter by some person or persons. Now while we feel very thankful for the disinterested kindness of friends, we wish them to give themselves no uneasiness on our account, as we feel perfectly competent to manage our own affairs, and wish not to hold them responsible for our doings. We would here say distinctly that no one besides ourself has any control over the columns of the Lily and we know not that we are controlled in our actions by any one. We may sometimes publish articles with the sentiments of which we do not fully agree, but we have the right, and shall fearlessly use it should occasion require, of expressing our disapprobation of any such sentiments.—Our readers must bear in mind that the Lily is a woman's paper, and one of its objects as stated in our prospectus is, *to open a medium through which woman's thoughts and aspirations might be developed*. Gentlemen have no reason to complain if women avail themselves of this medium, and here dare utter aloud their thoughts, and protest against the wrongs and grievances which have been so long heaped upon their sex.

When we look around us and see the extreme misery and degradation of many of our sex who were cradled in luxury and reared with care and tenderness—when we behold so many dragging out a wretched existence—mere slaves to men, who

Source: "Woman's Rights," *The Lily* 2, no. 4 (Apr. 1850).

in everything save physical strength are far inferior to them—when we see them toiling to earn a bare subsistence and then through fear and brutal force compelled to yield up the pittance they have earned, to idle and dissolute husbands—when we look upon the drunkard's wife and his scantily clothed and half starved children and witness their sufferings, we are more astonished that women have not long ere this arisen *en masse* and demanded their rights, and forcibly obtained them if they could not do so peacefully, than we are that a few should now, when opportunity offers, plead in behalf of their sorrowing sisters, and raise their united voices against the indignities to which they are subjected.

Women are awakening to a sense of their inferior position, and beginning to question the right of man to dictate laws for their observance—laws which they have no voice in making and at which their feelings revolt. They see that the evils which afflict society and which bear so heavily upon them are all the effects of these laws, and the question arises, "who gave man the right to make laws and sanction means calculated to oppress, degrade and render wretched woman's whole life?" They look in vain for an answer. If he has such authority it is only human. Divine law does not sanction it. God never designed man to be a tyrant, or woman to be a slave and bow to his dictates. We rejoice that the barriers to woman's equality are being thrown down, or overleaped; we are glad that she now has the press at her command, and may, if she will, stir up the mighty mass of people to give heed to her behests. We only wish there were more of them willing to devote their talents to the good of their sex, and the moral elevation of their race; and we can only hope that the spirit which has enkindled in the breasts of the few, may pervade the many, and that they may fully consider the part which it is their duty to take in arresting the terrible evils which have spread to such fearful extent over our beloved country.

"Have Women No Work To Do?"

THE LILY, April 1850

We often hear the remark from some of our own sex, when conversing with them upon the evils of intemperance, and the necessity of action on woman's part, "it is nothing that concerns us—it is men's business to tend to these matters, but women have no right to meddle with them." And is it really so? Have women nothing to do when their husbands and sons, fathers and brothers—yea, and mothers and sisters too, are year after year falling victims to the cruel and relentless destroyer? When they see those nearest and dearest to them cut down and destroyed without mercy—when the foe enters their dwellings and makes desolate their once happy firesides, must they fold their hands and sit at ease, waiting for *men* who have let loose this desolating scourge to curse the earth, to arise and crush it? No, no, it must not be. Woman has a duty to perform in this matter, and we believe she will be answerable to her Maker for the manner in which she discharges this duty. Men have too long dallied with the subject—they have too long played the fool while thirty thousand of their fellow beings are annually swept into the drunkard's grave.—They have too long made professions of deadly hostility against the foe, while their every act has been to fasten its deadly fangs more firmly upon community, for us to place much dependance on their ever subduing it without woman's aid and influence. We want something more than talk to convince us that men are sincere in their professions, and we want some better argument than men's efficiency to satisfy us that it is not woman's right and

Source: "Have Women No Work To Do?" *The Lily* 2, no. 4 (Apr. 1850).

duty to bring her influence to bear on this subject, and to nerve herself for a ceaseless conflict with the invader of her peace, and the destroyer of her happiness.

But it is not in behalf of her husband and sons alone, that woman's energies should be exerted. It is not man alone who is in danger, or who falls beneath the stroke of the destroyer. Women too, are its victims! Women—that portion of creation whom men pretend to guard with so much care, and shield from every rude blast—whom they dare not let speak or act for themselves, lest it should destroy their "soft and gentle natures." Yea, *women*, by thousands are corrupted, torn from their families, robbed of their virtue, derided, insulted, and driven forth inebriate outcasts to a life of prostitution, infamy, and crime, by this same scourge with which men have cursed the earth.

The legislative report shows that about 6,000 *intemperate women* have been confined in the jails of our State during the past year! This of course is but a small number of those who are addicted to the use of intoxicating drinks. And is not this enough to arouse the sympathies of women? Have they no part to take in staying this torrent of vice? Must they hesitate to enquire whether it is within their "sphere"? Nay, shall they not rather cast aside their blindness and folly, and by their future good works atone for their past indolence and carelessness? Up, sisters, to your duty! Fear not the jeers and frowns of men! Much, very much, rests upon you in this battle for human rights, and according as you faithfully discharge your duties, will be your reward, not only in this life, but also, we trust, in the life to come.

"Why Must Women Vote"

THE LILY, May 1850

Woman must exercise her right to the elective franchise and have her own representatives in our councils, for two great reasons.

1st. Man cannot represent us. He is thoroughly educated into the belief that woman's nature is altogether different from his own; he has no idea that she is governed by the same laws of mind with himself. Men, so far from viewing us like themselves, from their legislation, seem to think us their moral and intellectual antipodes in everything, for whatever law they consider good for themselves, they forthwith pass its opposite for us, and express the most profound astonishment, if we manifest the least dissatisfaction. For example: Our forefathers pitched King George, his authority, and his tea chests, all into the sea, because forsooth they were forced to pay taxes to British government, and yet had no representatives in their national councils. "Taxation without representation" was the text for many a hot debate in the forests of the new world, and for eloquent orations in the parliament of the old. Yet in forming a new government, the very rights were denied to us for which our fathers fought, and bled, and died to secure to themselves. They have not only taxed our property, but in many cases they take it all from us. They tax us to build colleges, then pass a special law forbidding any woman to enter there. A married woman is not supposed to have any legal existence. She has no more absolute rights than a slave on a southern plantation. She takes the name of her master, she owns noth-

Source: "Why Must Women Vote," *The Lily* 2, no. 5 (May 1850).

ing, she can get no redress for grievances in her own name in any court of justice this side of Heaven. The principle on which she is educated is the same. The slave is taught what is considered best for him to know,—which is nothing. The woman, what is best for her to know,—which is a little more than nothing,—man being the judge in both cases.—She cannot follow out the impulses of her own immortal mind in her sphere, any farther than the slave can in his. Civilly, socially and religiously, she is what man chooses her to be, nothing more or less,—and such is the slave, and this is slavery. It is impossible to convince man that we think and feel exactly as he does, that we have the same sense of right and wrong, the same love of justice, freedom and independence. Some regard us as angels and some as devils,—hence one class would shut us up in a certain sphere for fear of the evil that might be done us, and another for fear of the evil we might do; so, except for the sentiment in the matter, for all the good it does us, we might as well be the one as the other.

2d. Man cannot legislate for us. Our statute books and all past experience force this truth upon us. His laws made for our special benefit have been without exception unjust, cruel and aggressive. Having denied our identity with himself, he has no data to go upon in judging of our wants and interests. If we are alike in our mental structure, then certainly we ought to have a voice in making the laws which govern us,—if we are not alike, then we must make our own laws, as we alone can tell what we need. . . .

"Equality of Rights to Woman"

THE LILY, March 1852

In looking after the reasons which the advocates of Woman's exclusion from an equality of political rights have put forward as the grounds of the propriety of such exclusion, I will not venture to assert what they are or may be, but take them as already given not long since in a prominent political newspaper. They were there marshalled into three divisions, each of which was assumed to be sufficient to overwhelm opposition. First, that there was no considerable number of men in the country, who had confessed their inability to conduct the affairs of government as society and government are at present constituted. To this I will only say, we are not informed that George the III. ever confessed his inability to govern the American Colonies, nor have we any reason to believe that he ever doubted his ability. Yet our forefathers deliberately came to the conclusion that they would try to govern themselves without his assistance, and they as deliberately used the necessary means to secure the exercise of their choice of government. If the argument we are noticing be sound, they were guilty of a gross error. They should have submitted to the Royal will and pleasure of the House of Brunswick, until such time as it pleased that Royal House to confess its inability to govern.

The second reason is, that the women, excepting those who associate in the "Woman's Rights Conventions," are not ambitious to engage in the task of having a voice in the government to which they are subjected. I am not now ready to assent to the truth of this, nor shall I be, until they have had the oppor-

Source: "Equality of Rights to Woman, No. 7," *The Lily* 4, no. 3 (Mar. 1852).

tunity and refused to accept. Subdued, if not degraded, must be the character of those who will choose servitude of any kind in preference to freedom. It is not, like the first reason, new, but an old and very common stratagem of oppression, to make the world believe that its victims prefer their lot to any of the allurements, or advantages which liberty can furnish. The argument is really this; not that all bondage, or any specific kind of bondage, is justifiable, but that such a system or degree of bondage as crushes and annihilates all desire of freedom, is not only justifiable, but desirable. The assumption is, that women are in such bondage and of course always desire to remain so; therefore any attempt to cast off their servitude, or abate its severity, is high treason to the rights of the other sex. Now, if some women, or even a majority, prefer bondage to freedom and they are to have their choice, is that any reason, or any part of a reason, why those who choose freedom should be enslaved? It is true we live in a majority government, and where the majority rule, but there are many things which that majority cannot *rightfully* do; and among them, they cannot enslave the minority, or take from them the ordinary rights of citizenship. Otherwise, we should have a despotism, and neither its character would be changed, or its burdens lessened by the multitude of the despots.

The third and last reason, is the maternity argument and its consequences of the nursery.—And here allow me to quote the language, lest I may be charged of doing injustice to the author. He says: "If this system did not destroy the marriage relation and if woman's rights were not confined to spinsters, then under the new system we might expect women at certain times to appear under circumstances of embarrassment. The daily sittings of our courts would be interrupted to allow Judge, Jury, Suitor and Counsel to do those things, which in this less advanced age, are thought to be most suited to the nursery. Our military system would need amendments to enable officers and men, or rather women endeavoring to be men, before review or battle, to retire for nursery duty."

It appears that this maternity argument and its consequences, are regarded as the most troublesome obstacles to woman's rights, and the basis of all the claims to exclusiveness on the part of the aristocracy of sex. There are two reasons why we should treat it gently. Except a little aristocracy of "color," it is the only aristocracy left in our Bill of political franchises— and in those who use it, it betrays a verdancy, if not a juvenility that indicates a very recent and perhaps premature escape from the nursery and its ancillary accommodations.

The argument is, *some* women at *some* times could not conveniently perform the duties of Judge, Legislator and military commander, because of the duties of the nursery. Therefore *all* women should at *all* times be excluded from *all* political franchises: or in shorter form, because *some* women are and will be mothers, *all* women shall be nothing else. This is making maternity not merely an inconvenience, but a crime—inflicting the penalty not on the delinquents alone, but on all the sex alike—not only on one age, but on all ages. Some women may have been so inconsiderate as to have thought that the God of Nature had imposed physical ills on maternity sufficient to propitiate for any crime they were committing, without being excluded from the common rights of humanity as a further penalty for the sin of maternity. Now I would like to ask these fastidious gentlemen who have such recent and disagreeable recollections of the nursery, why they cannot just as well and in the same way, disfranchise the whole race, themselves included. Very few men can perform all of the various offices of government and none can do the whole at one and the same time. They are as frequently disabled by sickness as women, and because some are and all may be, why not on the same principle, exclude the whole from the rights of citizenship? If physical misfortunes are to produce political disabilities in the one sex, why not in the other? If maternity is a crime, these gentlemen are the results of crime, and "do men gather grapes of thorns, or figs of thistles?" It may be true that an individual is not to blame for being born, but I am yet to learn that there is any discrimination of sex in that respect.

The trouble in their reasoning is, the major proposition of their logic is all wrong. It assumes a principle utterly foreign to our political polity and every other, and equally abhorrent to common sense and common honesty. It is this, that every individual should be excluded from the common rights of citizenship, who is not capacitated to discharge and so circumstanced that he can discharge any and all official duties involved in the transactions of the government. Neither our government or any other ever recognized such a principle. But this is not the extent of the error in their premises. They have run their reasoning still further into the ground. Each and every individual of the same sex, must be so capacitated and circumstanced at any and all periods of life, beyond the possibility of even temporary interruption, or the whole are disfranchised. No proposition short of this in comprehension, would authorize their conclusion.

A question or two to these fastidious gentlemen and I have done with them and their namby-pamby arguments. If they are serious in their apprehensions of "circumstances of embarrassment" and inconvenience to result from the contingent liabilities of maternity in case women are allowed to appear in public as Judges and Jurors, why not similar apprehensions for their appearance in any other character? If from very propriety they are to be excluded in an official character, why not exclude them as witnesses and spectators? If from the Court House, why not from the churches and public and social assemblies of all descriptions?

"The American Costume"

THE LILY, March 1852

With women's rights already the subject of ridicule in many circles, the appearance of women wearing trousers proved too tempting a target for humor and too radical for the public taste. Even though the "bloomers" were eminently practical and not unattractive underneath the graceful knee-length skirts that covered them, they never caught on. Even the intrepid Elizabeth Cady Stanton finally gave up wearing them for fear the chorus of criticism would damage the cause of women's rights.

[We copy the following from the most respectable and even venerable authority, CHAMBER'S EDINBURGH JOURNAL:]

"So it is that our people see women every day defying common sense and good taste by the length of their skirts, and say little about it, but no sooner observe one or two examples of a dress verging a little too far in an opposite direction, than they raise the shout of a persecuting ridicule. We say there may be some little extravagance in the Bloomer idea, but it is common sense itself in comparison with the monstrous error and evil which it seeks to correct.

That some reform is wanted, all the male part of creation agree. Many of the ladies, too, admit the inconvenience of the long skirts which have been for some years in fashion, though they profess to be unable to break through the rule. Let there simply be a reduction of the present nuisance, an abbreviation

Source: "The American Costume," *The Lily* 4, no. 3 (Mar. 1852).

"Women's Emancipation." (Harper's New Monthly Magazine, *August 1851)*

of those trolloping skirts by which every man walking beside the wearer is not unfrequently defiled.

If the question is between the present skirts and Bloomerism, then we are Bloomerites; for we would rather consent to error in the right direction than the wrong one.

We have alluded to fashion and its slavery. It is a curious subject, not unworthy of even a philosophic attention. In the late wonderous exhibition of the industrial arts of the civilized world, how many admirable devices were presented for articles of utility and ornament! What an idea did it in its general effect give of the amount of ingenious intellect exercised on such matters! Yet we never see any of the same taste and ingenuity exercised in the fashioning of clothes. Milliners and tailors appear to be the most brainless of all professions. We scarcely remember to have seen a new fashion proceed from them which accorded with true elegance, and which did not tend to deform rather than adorn the human person. At present they make a woman into a bell-shaped object, painful from the sense of its incompleteness—feet being wanting. Always some absurdity reigns conspicuous in their models of form. Each of them will tell you: "We cannot help it—it is the fashion." But whence comes the fashion, if not from some of their own empty heads? And how is it that no one of them can help it, but that no one of them has the sense or spirit to devise, set forth, and promote anything better? The tailors are better than the milliners, and do not in general misdress mankind to such an extent as to call for a particular effort of resistance; but the women are treated by their dressmakers in a way which would call for and justify a rebellion. A friend of ours goes so far as to say that the one thing above all which convinces him of the inferiority of the female mind generally to the male, is the submission which women show to every foolish fashion which is dictated to them, and that helplessness which they profess under the most torturing and tyrannical rules.

"Dress Reform"

THE LILY, August 1852

We receive a great many letters similar to the following, and had we room should be glad to place them oftener before our readers. Wherever the reform dress has been adopted from principle, there it is still worn, and will continue to be, despite the opposition which may be felt to it.

NORTH MANCHESTER, Ind.

MRS. BLOOMER:—

I hope you will continue to devote a part of the paper to the reform in dress. This is too intimately connected with the elevation of woman to be neglected,—for in order that we may have sound minds in sound bodies, our dress must be such as to allow the full expansion of the chest, and the most perfect muscular development of the whole body. It is to be hoped that those women who have emancipated themselves from the thralldom of Parisian fashions, and braved the consequent censure of a wickedly depraved public sentiment, will continue in the way that leads to health and life. I am convinced that if women generally could be induced to adopt the new dress, after having tested its superiority they would be unwilling to resume the load of skirts they had carried for years.

Is it any wonder that the female constitution is becoming proverbially deteriorated, when we consider the enervating effects of the long, tight bodice, and the heavy skirts suspended from the hips.

A short time ago a lady, evidently suffering severely the

Source: "Dress Reform," *The Lily* 4, no. 8 (Aug. 1852).

Illustration of the "Bloomer costume" popularized in the 1850s dress reform movement. *(Courtesy: Women's Rights National Historical Park, Seneca Falls, N.Y.)*

penalty of the slave of fashion, said, on my remonstrating on her course, that she *"could not* change; for *she had worn stiff whale-bones so long that she could not support her body in an upright position without them."* And this is by no means an isolated case.

Thousands of women are in the same wretched situation,— and are such beings fit to transmit qualities to offspring—fit to be the mothers of our future rulers and statesman? This is one great reason why the organization of so many infants is so imperfect that they must either fall into untimely graves, or continue an existence which is little better than a curse to its possessor.

This state of things calls loudly for a reformation in the

form of dress; and all women who would secure the health and consequent happiness of themselves and their offspring are in *duty bound* to investigate the subject, and fashion their dress according to the dictates of *reason* and *common sense*.

There are some half dozen here who wear the reform dress, and I hope more will yet be induced to take an interest in it. . . .

MARY F. THOMAS.

FLORA HILL, Mich., July 22, 1852.

MRS. BLOOMER—DEAR MADAM:—I thank you for the stand you have taken in the dress reform, and feel it my duty to add my little encouragement. If from all parts where this reform is at work you should receive the same, you would have, I think, no cause for despondency. The new costume is advancing steadily, not rapidly, but I think surely, here; yet I might say rapidly, for where twelve months ago it was only known as a thing to be, it is now an every-day occurrence.

It is not found in the aristocratic circles! Who ever heard of a reform to benefit mankind beginning there? They cannot originate one, or even follow one that has been originated, until it becomes popular, and they are compelled to fall into its wake or be left in the darkness of the past. To do otherwise would be to act counter to the very thing, (I cannot call it principle) that has placed them where they are, and in accordance with which, they continue to fill those stations.

A person to be popular, must bow to what popularity demands; and they who are too truth-loving and intelligent to do this, cannot occupy these exalted (?) places: neither would they.—They feel that it would be a degradation to their humanity to be applauded by such as worship this fashion-god,—this aristocratic, popular deity. It is this latter class of men and women that you find adopting the reforms of the day. They love not a thing because it is old—nor should they; for age can never make a falsehood true, or an evil a good; but they love truth for its own sake, not for its age, whether it be old or young; and if it be a truth that short dresses and close good fitting trowsers are more convenient, healthy, and modest than the

> Ample skirt of flowing breadth
> That trails through dust and mire;

and in mounting a flight of steps, or into a carriage requires both hands to keep it from under the feet and preciptating its wearer to the ground, then they wish to receive it, and act accordingly; and this is the conviction of those that have tried the two styles of dress.

But aristocratic friends say, "Do not put them on yet, they will one day become popular—they must, for they are decidedly more convenient, and custom will make them appear far more becoming; but it will not do to wear them till they do become so, for it will make you appear ridiculous!" Now how in reason is this to be brought about if all act on this one idea of popularity?

It is not the ignorant class, that adopt the reform dress, for either they ape as far as possible the aristocracy, or cling to what was in existence at the time of their birth; for their intellect has not advanced much since that period, and their habits could hardly stride ahead of it! Rest assured it is an intelligent class, acting on the principles of a truthful conviction that have ventured to stand the haughty frown of popularity, or the indecent sneer of vulgar ignorance, and, in freedom, appear before the world in the "New Costume." Truly yours,   E. P. B.

*   *   *

LATEST FASHION.—We are sorry to see that the old fashioned big sleeves are again coming into favor. These are much more offensive to our taste than the short skirt and trousers, and we hope they may not become general; yet we are willing that all should wear them who choose, and—we shall not feel called upon to treat those who follow this fashion with ridicule or insult.

"Letter from Mrs. Stanton to the Woman's Temperance Convention"

THE LILY, March 1852

DEAR FRIENDS:—Though I cannot be present with you to take part in your deliberations at the coming convention, yet I take great pleasure in sending you a letter expressive of the deep interest I feel in your efforts in the cause of Temperance. I hail any movement on the part of woman that shows the coming up of the active principle within—a determination in her to remedy the evils she has so long supinely endured. The true reformer has two great works that should be carried on at the same time. One is to mollify and relieve the sufferings caused by existing evils; the other, and far higher work, is to prevent their recurrence by seeking out, and removing, if possible, their causes. The one is superficial and fragmentary; the other goes to the depths of the spiritual existence of man. For our present outward work I would suggest two points for your consideration.

1st. The importance to this cause that woman exercise her right to the elective franchise. Inasmuch as this monster Intemperance is in part a creature of law, we who are its innocent victims ought surely to have a voice in putting him down.

2nd. It is our sacred duty to create a new public sentiment in regard to the marriage obligations of Drunkards' wives. We must raise a higher standard of virtue, heroism, and true womanhood. Heretofore, it has been thought the duty of woman to love, honor and obey her husband, no matter what his transformation might be, from the lover, to a tyrant, licentiate or beast. And loud and long have been the praises bestowed on those wives who have loved and lived on, in filth, poverty and rags,

Source: "Letter from Mrs. Stanton," *The Lily* 4, no. 3 (Mar. 1852).

the wretched companion of a drunkard's sorrows, and the more wretched mother of his ill starred children.

Alas! how many excellent women have dragged out a weary existence in such a partnerhip, from mistaken ideas of duty—from a false sense of religious obligation?

Think you *God* ever joined together virtue and vice—purity and obscenity—a soul of heavenly aspirations, with a creature of the lower appetites? No! never!!

It is love and sympathy alone that constitutes and sanctifies true marriage, and any woman sacrifices her claims to virtue and nobility, who consents to live in the relation of wife with any man, whom she has ceased to love and respect. Such companionship, call it what you may, is nothing more or less than legalized licentiousness.

Let us encourage—yea, urge those stricken ones, who are kept down by crude notions of God's laws, and the tyranny of a false public sentiment, to sunder those unholy ties, to save themselves from such debasing contact, and to escape the guilt of stamping on the brow of innocence, a nature so low and carnal as is that of the confirmed drunkard. But what is the cause of drunkenness, licentiousness and gluttony—for all these are but different manifestations of the same internal malady. Is it not the preponderance of the animal over the spiritual nature? And so long as by the excessive self-indulgence of our times, we continue to cultivate this already overgrown animal nature, we must look for the continuance of these vices.

Could we change the form of the vice, and make all men gluttons, rather than drunkards, what essential service have we performed for the race? What better are brains, befogged with meats and pastry, than those enlivened by rum?

If we would now begin a lasting work—if we would take onward steps that need never be retraced, we must give up our idle, luxurious habits, and begin a life of self-denial and activity. Let us but cultivate the *spiritual* in ourselves and children, with half the assiduity we have the animal, and we shall soon see a mighty change in our midst. It is not in Conventions, dear friends, that our best work begins.

The radical reform must start in our homes, in our nurseries, in ourselves.

Temperance Notes

THE LILY, August 1852

We hear good reports from the agents of the Woman's State Temperance Society, who are now lecturing in Western New York. They are every where well received, and auxiliaries to the State Society are being formed in many sections. There seems to be a general response to the sentiments of the Woman's Temperance convention held in April last. From all parts we are receiving letters bearing thanks, and the utterance of joyful feelings over the proceedings of that meeting. A chord was then touched that will long continue to vibrate. Woman's spirit is stirred with new hopes, new desires, and strong determinations for the future; and there is promise that the good seed then sown will tell upon the public mind, and produce, in good time, an abundant havest.

We learn from the Cayuga Chief that the wife of a certain drunken Judge in Wayne Co., has taken her rights into her own hands and made a general smash of the bar-room furniture of the drunkery where her husband got his liquor—nor did she forget to deal a few blows over the head of the rumseller. The name of this woman is not given, which we much regret. Such women are an honor to their sex and entitled to public praise. We hope when she got the drunken Judge home she did not forget to give him a few lashes too. He deserved them as much as the rumseller.

There will be a convention of women at Syracuse, N.Y., on the 8th, 9th, and 10th of September. It is hoped that the friends of equal rights will turn out in large numbers.

Source: The Lily 4, no. 8 (Aug. 1852).

"Letter from Mrs. Gage"

THE LILY, August 1852

Frances Dana Gage, an Ohio feminist, abolitionist, and mother of eight, was a frequent contributor to the popular press in the 1850s.

DEAR MRS. BLOOMER:—You have been made aware ere this that I attended the Woman's Rights Conventions held in Ohio and Pennsylvania. As these Conventions have been so well discussed through the papers, it would be idle for me to say anything of either, as conventions; but it may not be amiss to give my thoughts as to the results of such general meetings.

I have never been able to see clearly any objection to Woman's Rights Conventions which may not be urged against any other gathering of the people, for any other object.

We honestly believe that the subject of the elevation of woman is one of vital importance to community. We know and feel that our views are ultra, in the common acceptation of the term. We know, too, that we are misunderstood, and misrepresented. We endeavor in all ways practicable to spread our views and feelings around us at home; but the home circle is small and our voices reach not beyond our own neighborhood. We are isolated, in many cases, and so few in number, struggling against such fearful odds, that we grow weary, faint of heart, and relax our energy. We long to meet sympathisers—to see others who think as we think, feel as we feel—are ready for truth's sake to take an unpopular position before the world. We long, too, to unite our influence, to give forth to the world evi-

Source: "Letter from Mrs. Gage," *The Lily* 4, no. 8 (Aug. 1852).

dence of our devotion to truth—to call its attention, by speaking to it through our conventions with an united voice, instead of sending out here and there a solitary note—to startle it with our loud cry for right and justice.

Our opponents give us a great deal of good advice—for which, as it costs nothing, I suppose we are in duty bound to be thankful—about "keeping within our sphere," "doing home duty," "keeping out of brawls, and preserving our woman's nature"—and so forth, and so on. All this may be needed to keep woman from becoming—what?—can any one tell? *I* cannot; and I must say so far as I know the reformers as a class there is no class that live out all the duties of true women more fully than they. If there springs up an erratic genius among us, here and there, who chooses to do unseemly things, and think unseemly thoughts, the cause which we advocate is in no way responsible for their oddities; nor are we bound to endorse their idiosyncracies. A murderer may advocate mercy and justice; a thief lecture upon honesty and fair dealing, and the debauchee preach sermons upon temperance and virtue. The *truth* is the same, and mercy, justice, honesty and virtue as binding in their allegation upon every human heart, as if all their advocates lived up to their high and holy teachings.

The idea that a woman cannot go from home for a week to attend a convention without neglecting duties is to me very strange indeed. Can she leave home for a week for any cause without being liable to the same charge? Who has a right to decide whether she shall spend a week or a month of absence from home, in visiting friends, going to Saratoga, Newport or Minnesota—attending meetings of the Presbytery, Synod, Methodist conference, or camp-meeting—whether she shall take a trip to Niagara, the capital, or a Woman's Rights Convention? Who has a right to be the keeper of any woman's conscience? If she settles her account with husband, children, and friends at home, violates no law of the land, outrages no principle of right, who has any right to say she may not carry out her own convictions and inclinations?

This defence of conventions may seem to you entirely uncalled for; but I find very many people who feel the necessity of doing something for the elevation of our sex, and the race, who shrink from making any effort beyond the charmed circle of domestic life. I would have them do all duty there, and then, if there be a talent to be used beyond that, I would say to them in empathic language, "roll not your talent in a napkin"—"put not your light under a bushel." If you have a truth to utter that will do good to *ten* around the family altar, and you have the ability to make that truth heard by *thousands,* it is your right and duty to speak it to the thousands, and the thousands will be benefitted.

But I must not tarry longer to discuss conventions. I rather guess we shall hold them now and then, in spite of conservatism; and if they increase in popular favor as they have done, our opponents will have to get up Anti-Woman's Rights conventions to counteract our influence; and then we shall have the pro and con of the whole matter before the public. But now to my journey.

Really, there are so many things that I want to talk about that I hardly know what to talk of first. Perhaps it should be of the kindness and gallantry of the rail-road companies, who allowed us crazy disorganizers to whirl over their routes at half price. Surely we owe them many thanks, and I earnestly hope that other states may follow their example and secure our good will by laying us under similar pleasant obligations. Permit me here to remark, that traveling from my home to Philadelphia, and back, without the protection of a gentleman, has tended to improve my ideas of mankind in general, and actually to make me doubt their own averments that they are all rude, uncivilized, and that a lady should always have a male protector in traveling.

A protector against what? Against men of course—there are no wild beasts in the way nowadays to be protected against. I did not, in one instance, say to conductor, stage agent, or steamboat captain that I was alone and would be thankful for kindness; but it was as cheerfully, kindly and respectfully bestowed, as if I had been an own aunt. Protectors and traveling companions! why I could have a dozen of both sexes, any time I want, from home, *if convenient;* but if not, and it is necessary that I should go alone, I would wish to be able to do it, and to have every other woman do the same without fear or annoyance. I would have every woman taught self-reliance as well as virtue; for there are but few in this world who do not find it necessary at some time in life to meet with trial and difficulty—who find themselves placed where necessity requires they should act alone. Let every woman fit herself for the emergencies of life,—if they never come, well and good; but if they do, her advantage is incalculable.

I was introduced by Mrs. M. A. W. Johnson, who traveled with me from Massillon to Philadelphia, into the family of James and Lucretia Mott, who gave me a sister's welcome to their home. This excellent couple are well known to the world, and need no word of praise from me; but I want to add my mite, and so I will. If all fathers and mothers, husbands and wives, church members and citizens of this our republic were as good as James and Lucretia Mott, we reformers would have nothing to do beyond the dooryard gate. The world would be good enough, plenty. There would be no war, no slavery, no intemperance, no licentiousness, no crime, no wrong. Ha! what a world it would be!

The day after our arrival we visited among other things, Mrs. Sarah Tyndale's great china store—said to contain the greatest variety of china and porcelain collected in any one establishment in the country. It has been under the care and supervision of a woman for years. If one woman can do this, cannot another? Let those who are working at sewing, or housework for one dollar per week try it, and see if they cannot better their condition. Mrs. Tyndale has not been idle in the great works of reform, while devoting herself to business. The moral reforms of the city, and the anti-slavery cause, have found her a fast friend. . . .

From Mrs. Tyndale's, my companions—Mrs. Mott, and Dr. Harriet K. Hunt of Boston—went directly to the residence of Mrs. Sarah J. Hale; with whom Dr. Hunt wished an interview; and I of course was glad of an opportunity to look into the face of one who for years had delighted me with her thoughts, so I accompanied them. Mrs. Hale is a very pleasant looking woman, with a very polished manner; and if she receives every one as she did us, I should say kind and cordial. She does not seem to look with favor upon our woman's rights movements, our conventions, &c. Sorry I am for it, for her name and influence would do us much good.—Yet while I would be glad to give her a welcome into our ranks, I feel no disposition to find fault with her for not being there. She is opposed, I believe, also to educating the male and female mind together, and is now using her influence for the benefit of the Female Medical College of Pennsylvania. This is an institution for women only. I have never been able, as yet, to discover the necessity of educating apart, those whose practical duties in life must be acted out together. Why is it not as modest and proper for a woman to be Dr. as patient? Can any one tell? But, as I said before, I find no fault with them for their position. *They* see things from one stand point, *I* from another. Let us each do our work honestly, and all will yet be well. If others will not go with us, let us speed them on their journey in their own way if the path they pursue will lead at last to the wished-for goal.

Mrs. Hale is also petitioning Congress for a grant of land, for the purpose of educating female teachers. This is a great idea. Surely it is time that one half of the tax-payers, and all of the mothers of the other half should be helped a little by the government in fitting themselves to rear and educate men—the future lords and statesmen who are to rule the world—saying nothing about *the women, who always rule the rulers,* you know.

One word of Dr. Hunt, and I will close this long letter. This lady has been some eighteen years a medical adviser in Boston, and has made for herself not only a competence, but a luxurious home, and a pleasant independence.

If I was sick I should like to have such a cheerful and kind hearted doctor; and, I think her ringing child-like laugh would do a dispeptic more good than a round bushel of tomato pills, or a gallon of *Pepsin.* May we have more like her ere long, to heal the hearts as well as the bodies of poor suffering humanity.

But farewell for to-day,
AUNT FANNY.

"The *Democratic Review* on Woman's Rights"

THE LILY, August 1852

The starving millions of Europe, in America find ample rewards for their industry, broad acres, and in due time, their "cattle upon a thousand hills." It is no vainglorious boast, that we have room enough and resources enough to furnish a just recompense to labor, no matter from what country, or of what race, comes the laborer. The addition of millions of foreign operatives to our working strength has not in the least diminished the compensation of individual labor, or lessened its demand. All these facts add to the meanness of the spirit which sustains the dogma of woman's restriction in her industrial occupations, in order to improve by contrast the apparent position of the other sex. It is obvious, that if the great influx of foreign laborers has not diminished individual opportunities, opening wide the door to all womankind, would not produce such an effect.—It would truly be, as the Review expresses it, only dragging "down man from the high position which nature and necessity assign to him," by leveling up woman; despoiling him of his greatness by contrast; of his felicity by the miseries of others; cheating the sympathies of the world by robbing them of the opportunity of enhancement on the death of a father, or a brother, by the announcement that a wife and children, or a mother and half a dozen sisters, were thereby deprived of their sole support....

Some men are vain and simple enough to satisfy them-

Source: "The Democratic Review on Woman's Rights.—No. 5." *The Lily* 4, no. 8 (Aug. 1852).

selves, that woman's mode of dress and the round of her avocations have been fixed by a certain degree of mental and bodily
imbecility, which never overtakes the other sex. They seem not
to perceive and probably never will, for a reason obvious to all
not as simple as themselves, that if a certain degree of weakness is to be the line of long skirts, they are themselves tres-
passing on forbidden ground; and instead of exposing their
nether extremities in bifurcated garments they should fall into
rank in proper costume, at the same time giving way to the
women who are stronger, to put on the dress which by the rule
of their own adoption they never had any right to wear.

But the hero of the Review further comes down in battle
array upon the Bloomer costume and woman's rights of industry, assuming more sacred panoply. After incorporating in its
creed the fixed faith of her debasement and subordination,
and establishing to its own satisfaction, the rectitude of both
by "dogma," "command" and "mystery," the wondering multitude might have been pardonable for believing that Mahomet
had been to the mountain, or the mountain had been to Mahomet, and that this was the conjoint product of their consequent
groans and labors; that all else pertaining to female polity,
social, domestic, industrial and political, had been conferred to
man's domination, without provision in the Creator's constitution, or ordinance of Christianity, encompassing the limits of
woman's avocations, or fixing the length of her petticoats. But
with the Review for authority, not even these details have been
left to man, but presecribed and the fashion-plate given in the
book of Nature and Revelation. Hear it. "Must we have women
brazening the stare of the mob in Bloomer costume? meeting
in public rooms to declare their contempt of Christian obligations and their fitness for masculine avocations? openly denouncing the law of God, written not more strongly in the
revealed will than in sex, with all its inevitable necessity and
inviolable destiny, its heavy responsibilities and vital duties?"

For this concession, that to Heaven and not to man, woman
is to look for directions as to the length and fashion of her
clothing and the mode of industry by which she is to gain her
bread and butter, she cannot feel too grateful; for it is possible,

that if her dress should at times fall short an inch or two of the prescribed length, or if she should now and then save herself and family from starvation by attempting what are called masculine avocations, she might make her peace with the former; but with the old fogies whom the Review assumes to personate, in the mountains and in the tombs crying and cutting themselves with stones because of the woman's rights agitation, never.

The spasmodic exhibitions of holy horrors and sanctimonious imprecations on the part of old fogydom, are more ridiculous than serious; more disgusting than terrible, without even the merit of novelty. Nothing is more common than for hardened old sinners, stale in crime and corruption, to discourse about Christian virtues, and deprecate the vices with which they have been bloated all their days. And as those who rule nations lay claim to the right divine of kings, we must expect the more petty incumbents of domestic tyranny will be apish enough to base their pretensions upon something of similar character, equally absurd.

In one particular however, the Review in its spirit of injustice and cowardly cruelty, darkens the shadows of the past and outsteps all contemporaries, except perhaps, the woman-whipper of Austria. To the fury of the mob it would expose woman and at the same time deny her even the safety of flight. It is plain, that the sin charged, is not in the mob: that belongs to masculine dignity; it is not in the "brazening;" though that would be naughty, she should be more humble; it is in the Bloomer costume; in being dressed with the facility for fight or flight. The Nero's and Caligula's have generally been content with exposing their fellow creatures to the fury of wild beasts, or of still wilder men, armed for defence, or with the chance of escape. Never before was it claimed that Nature's God required that anything in his own image should be so periled in defenceless, helpless condition. And if men must exhibit their prowess in mobbing women, who, that is capable of a generous impulse, except him of the Review, will deny to the latter the privilege of meeting such perils, not only in Bloomer costume, if they choose, but with a revolver in a practiced hand!

Short Items

THE LILY, August 1852

ATTICA, May 19th, 1852.

MRS. BLOOMER:—I write you by request of the Sisters of Dew-Drop Union, to express to you the deep interest they have felt in the perusal of the May No. of your valuable paper containing an account of the Convention at Rochester. This was a bold and courageous effort of the Women, and the best calculated to convince the people that they are in right good earnest and *invincible*. Most of the sentiments advanced at this meeting met with a ready response in each one of our hearts. We feel an increasing interest on this great subject and wish to contribute in a greater degree to the furtherance of the cause; but all our efforts have been productive of but little good at present. No doubt we are helping to bring about a change in public sentiment, which alone will remove many obstacles and render the work easy, pleasant and effectual.

We wish you to send to Dew-Drop Union two copies of The Lily, for one year, for which we enclose $1. It is just such a paper as is needed at the present time. In this, Woman can speak without restraint, and eventually her voice will be heard. Such unity and determination of purpose on the part of Woman, to free her country from the thraldom of Intemperance, must result in victory.

Yours in the bonds of Virtue, Love and Temperance.

JULIET L. DORRANCE, R.S.

* * *

Source: The Lily 4, no. 8 (Aug. 1852).

Speaking of a recent Woman's Rights Convention, an exchange remarks:—

In the way of governing, however, it strikes us that the very remarkable error made by the first woman in assuming the direction of things, should admonish the sex of their true weakness.

To this 'one of Eve's daughters' replies:—

As regards the 'remarkable error' alluded to in the paragraph, one would suppose that man had as little to boast of as woman, in that affair, seeing that he proved himself equally weak in resisting temptation, and added to his weakness the *meanness* of being a *tell-tale;* they were therefore placed pretty nearly on an equality, except that woman had some advantage in point of generosity, which we are willing to waive, insisting only on *Equality of Rights.*

*   *   *

"WE HAVE THEM NOW!—Among the resolutions passed at the Westchester Woman's Rights Convention was the following:

Resolved, That if it be true, that it is woman's province to soothe the angry passions and calm the belligerent feelings of man, we know of no place where she would find a riper harvest awaiting her labor, than in the halls of our National and State Legislatures.

PART
4

THE MOMENTUM: WOMEN'S RIGHTS CONVENTIONS AFTER SENECA FALLS

Rochester, New York, 1848

"Woman's Rights Convention"

At a Convention, held in the Unitarian Church in the city of Rochester, on the 2d day of August, 1848, to consider the Rights of Women: politically, socially, religiously, and industriously.

AMY POST, called the meeting to order and reported on behalf of the Committee, the following persons to serve as officers: ABIGAIL BUSH, President; LAURA MURRAY, Vice President; CATHARINE A. F. STEBBINS, SARAH L. HALLOWELL, and MARY H. HALLOWELL, Secretaries.

Prayer by Rev. Mr. WHICHER.

The minutes of the preliminary meeting, were then read; at which time, some anxiety was manifest concerning the low voices of the women, and when reading or speaking was attempted, cries of louder, louder, nearly drowned them, without giving time for adapting them to the size of the house; and the President remarked that "we presented ourselves there before them as an oppressed class, with trembling frames and faltering tongues, and we did not expect to be able to speak so as to be heard by all at first; but she trusted we should have the sympathy of the audience, and that they would bear with our weakness, now in the infancy as we were of the movement; that our trust in the omnipotency of right was our only faith that we should succeed."

W. C. NELL then read an address highly commendatory of the energies and rare devotion of women in every good cause,

Source: "Woman's Rights Convention," *The North Star* 1, no. 33 (11 Aug. 1848).

illustrated by facts in proof of her equality with man—adding that he "should never cease to award the grateful homage of his heart for their zeal, in behalf of the oppressed class with which he stood identified."

LUCRETIA MOTT, said she must be allowed to object to some portions of it, such as calling woman the better half of creation &c.,—man had become so accustomed to speak of woman in the language of flattering compliments, that he indulges in it unaware that there are some evidences of improvement—instance the reform in the literature of the day—the sickly sentimentality of the "Ladies Department," is fast disappearing, it being perceived that her mind requires more substantial food.—She also objected to calling man a tyrant, it is power that makes him tyrannical, and woman is equally so when she has irresponsible power. We shall not place woman in a true position until we form a just estimate of mankind as created by God.

WILLIAM C. NELL, disclaimed all intention to flattery, he did not think that flattery, which is spoken in truth.

A letter from GERRIT SMITH was read expressing his deep interest in the objects of the convention, and regreting his inability to be present.

The following declaration of sentiments, adopted at the Seneca Falls Convention, was submitted.... [See "Declaration of Sentiments," pp. 85–88.]

The expression of Sentiment on this Declaration being invited by the President, ELIZABETH C. STANTON, hoped the invitation would be accepted, and desired opposers would be more generous than to withhold objections until the convention was dispersed—as at Seneca Falls, where the ministers reviewed it in their pulpits on the Sabbath day....

Mr. CONKLIN of New Haven, felt great interest in the cause, saying "he loved the ladies as well as they love themselves," but he would not have woman exceed her proper sphere; he thought her place was at home; it was her empire and her throne—should deprecate exceedingly her occupying the pulpit.

L. MOTT said, he represented a large class of community

whose education had led them to limit the sphere of woman—
she desired him to read his Bible again and see if there is anything there to prohibit her being a religious teacher, though it
was not strange that he had initiated such views coming as he
did, from New Haven, Conn.; said we had derived our views
too much from the Clergy instead of the Bible.

Hon. W. C. Bloss, admitted that good results would attend
the exercise of the elective franchise by woman, but portrayed
many obstacles in the path of that reform, and inquired if there
was not a natural disqualification; did not boys and girls
exhibit dissimilarity of taste in the choice of play-things, the
one preferring the noisy hammer or the hoop, and the other the
darling doll at home; and were not these same traits only more
fully developed in after life?

Rebecca M. M. Sanford of Ann Arbor, eloquently advocated
the just claim of woman to an equality with man. Her remarks
were listened to with close attention and produced a marked
impression upon the audience.

At the request of L. Mott, Elizabeth M'Clintock read some
lines from the pen of Mariah W. Chapman, styled "The Times
that try Men's Souls," and signed "Lords of Creation," in reply
to a pastoral letter written some years since.

M. D. Codding objected to that part of the declaration in
regard to political action, he thought it sufficient for women to
vote through their fathers, husbands, and brothers, but concluded by wishing them a hearty God speed! He was asked
whether he voted by proxy, that he thought it so desirable for
women?

Frederick Douglass remarked, that the only true basis of
rights, was the capacity of individuals, and as for himself he
dared not claim a right which he would not concede to women.
In reference to the enfranchisement of women, it need not be
questioned whether she would use that right or not; he contended, that man should not withhold it from her; he alluded
to the oppressive customs in the Old World, which so wronged
woman, that they subjected her to the most laborious as well
as degrading means for a livelihood. He would see her elevated
to an equal position with man in every relation of life.

AFTERNOON SESSION.

A large audience convened. Opportunity for prayer was given. A long and interesting letter from JAMES C. JACKSON, approving the objects of the convention was read.

SARAH C. OWEN then presented an address portraying the evils to which women are subject.

SARAH D. FISH, also read an address setting forth some of the causes of woman's degradation, and urging her earnestly to come forward to the work of elevation. Several resolutions were read, which L. MOTT ably advocated; though she thought them too tame—she wanted something more stirring.

Mrs. ROBERTS reported the average price of labor for semp-stresses to be from 31 to 38 cts per day, board from $1.25 to $1.50 per week to be deducted therefrom, and they are generally obliged to take half or more than half in due bills.

Mrs. GAWLEY, corroborated the statement, having herself experienced some of the oppression of this portion of our citizens, and expressed her gratitude that the subject was claiming attention.

Mrs. STANTON, offered a resolution respecting the wages of house servants, which she thought too low for the labor they perform, and urged the necessity of reformers commencing at home.

Mrs. MOTT said, our aim should be to elevate the lowly and aid the weak. She compared the condition of woman with that of the free colored population, and dwelt upon the progress they had made within the past few years, urging imitation of their perseverance through opposition and prejudice—and said, while woman is regarded as an inferior being—while the Bible is brought forward to prove the right of her present position, and while she is disposed to feel satisfied with it, all these efforts can do but little. We cannot expect to do much by meeting in convention for those borne down by the oppressor, unless the oppressed *themselves feel* and *act;* and while so little attention is paid to education, and so little respect to woman. She spoke of the education of boys and girls in England. The common schools for boys show an improvement, mathematics and many of the higher branches being taught; while the girls learn little more than to read, write and keep their little accounts—sewing being the principal object of attention. The teachers say it will not do to educate them, "you unfit them for servants." We grant, that woman's intellect is feeble because she has been so long crushed. Does one man have fewer rights than another, because his intellect is inferior? if not, why should woman be denied her rights for that reason? Let her arise and demand them, and in a few years we shall see a different mental development.—She regarded this as the beginning of the day when woman shall rise, when she shall occupy her appropriate position in society.

Many pertinent remarks were made by E. C. STANTON, RHODA DEGARMO and ANN EDGWORTH.

ELIZABETH W. M'CLINTOCK, read some notes taken of a sermon preached at Seneca Falls, Sunday following the Convention held there, reviewing their declaration of sentiments, to which ELIZABETH C. STANTON, made an able reply.

The meeting adjourned until 7 o'clock.

EVENING SESSION.

The Declaration of Sentiments was again read, and 107 signatures obtained.

Mr. SULLY wished to ask fathers if they had considered this subject—what effect this equality would have on the happiness of a family if the wife and husband should differ in regard to politics or the education of a child? Mrs. MOTT replied by asking, "Which is preferable, ignorant or intelligent differences?"—Mr. SULLY further said, When the two heads disagree, who must *decide*?—There is no Lord Chancellor to whom to apply; but does not St. Paul strictly enjoin obedience to husbands, and that man shall be head of the woman? Mrs. MOTT replied, that in an extensive intercourse with the Society of Friends, she had never known any difficulty to arise on account of the wife's not having promised obedience in the marriage contract. She had never known any other mode of decision except a resort to argument, an appeal to reason; and although in some of the meetings of this society, women are placed on an equality, none of the results so much dreaded have occurred. The opposers of women's rights, who, though they bid us obey the bachelor St. Paul, themselves reject his counsel—he advised them not to marry. In general answer, she would quote, "One is your master, even Christ." Although Paul enjoins silence on women in the church, yet he gives directions how they should appear when they *are* speaking; and we have scriptural accounts of honorable women not a few who were religious teachers—Phebe, Priscilla, Tryphena, Tryphosa, and the four daughters of Philip, and various others.

Mrs. STANTON thought the gentleman could be easily answered: the strongest will or the superior intellect now govern the household as they will in the new order; she knew many a woman who to all intents and purposes, is at the head of her family.

The resolutions were then read, and AMY POST moved their adoption. A discussion ensued, in which Mrs. MOTT, Mrs. STANTON, and Mr. PICKARD, participated.

Mr. PICKARD asked, Who, after marriage, should hold property, and whose name should be retained? He thought an umpire necessary; all business must cease until the consent of both parties be obtained. He saw an impossibility of introducing such a rule into society. The gospel has established the unity of the married pair—they two are one.

Mrs. STANTON thought property might be held jointly, and the choice of names discretionary with the parties. The custom of taking the husband's name is not universal.

The following resolutions were now adopted, with but two or three dissenting voices:

Resolved, That we petition our State Legislature for our right to the elective franchise, every year, until our prayer be granted.

Resolved, That it is an admitted principle of the American Republic, that the only just power of government is derived from the consent of the governed; and that taxation and representation are inseparable; and woman being taxed equally with man, therefore she ought not to be deprived of an equal representation in the government.

Resolved, That we greatly deplore the apathy and indifference of woman in regard to her rights. It restricts her to the occupancy of an inferior religious, political and domestic station in society; and we wish to inspire her with a desire to stand on an equal basis, claiming her equal right to think, speak and act on all subjects that interest the human family.

Resolved, That the assumption of law to settle estates, when men die without wills, leaving widows, is an insult to woman, and ought to be regarded as such by every friend of right and humanity.

Resolved, That in the persevering and independent course of Mrs. BLACKWELL, who recently attended a series of medical lectures at Geneva, and has now gone to Europe to graduate as a physician, we see a harbinger of a day when woman shall stand forth, "redeemed and disenthralled," and perform those important duties which are so truly within her sphere.

Whereas, the husband has the legal right to hire out his wife to service, collect her wages, and appropriate them to his exclusive or independent benefit; and whereas, this has contributed to establish that hideous custom, the promise of obedience in the marriage contract, effectually, though insidiously, reducing her almost to the condition of a slave, whatever freedom she may have being granted her as a privilege, not as a right: therefore,

Resolved, That we will seek the overthrow of the barbarous and unrighteous law, and encourage woman no longer to promise obedience in the marriage contract.

Resolved, That the universal doctrine of the inferiority of woman, has ever caused her to distrust her own powers, and paralyzed her energies, and placed her in that diffident position which requires the most strenuous and unremiting efforts to overcome, but which will be effected by faithful perseverance in the practical exercise of those talents so long "wrapped in a napkin and buried in the earth."

Resolved, That those who think the laboring class of women are oppressed, ought to do all in their power to raise their wages, beginning with their own household servants.

Resolved, That we tender a vote of thanks to the Trustees

of the Unitarian Church, for kindly granting the use of it to this Convention.

Resolved, That the friends interested in this movement gratefully accept the kind offer of the Trustees of Protection Hall to hold our meetings whenever we choose.

Worcester, Massachusetts, 1850, 1851

As the enthusiasm for women's rights spread among like minds, so did conventions devoted to the cause. The following announcement, or "Call" as it was termed, summoned the women—and men—of Worcester and surrounding communities to take up the banner of women's rights. It is a statement whose tone, as one feminist said, was one of "modesty and moderation," but in its denunciation of the "tyranny which degrades and crushes wives and mothers," it is nonetheless a ringing call to action.

THE CALL

A Convention will be held at Worcester, Mass., on the 23d and 24th of October next, to consider the question of Woman's Rights, Duties, and Relations. The men and women who feel sufficient interest in the subject to give an earnest thought and effective effort to its rightful adjustment, are invited to meet each other in free conference at the time and place appointed.

The upward tending spirit of the age, busy in an hundred forms of effort for the world's redemption from the sins and sufferings which oppress it, has brought this one, which yields to none in importance and urgency, into distinguished prominence. One-half the race are its immediate objects, and the

Source: Elizabeth Cady Stanton, Susan B. Anthony et al., *The History of Woman Suffrage* (6 vols.; New York, 1881–1922; reprint, New York, 1969), vol. 1.

other half are as deeply involved, by that absolute unity of interest and destiny which Nature has established between them. The neighbor is near enough to involve every human being in a general equality of rights and community of interests; but men and women in their reciprocities of love and duty, are one flesh and one blood; mother, sister, wife, and daughter come so near the heart and mind of every man, that they must be either his blessing or his bane. Where there is such mutuality of interests, such an interlinking of life, there can be no real antagonism of position and action. The sexes should not, for any reason or by any chance, take hostile attitudes toward each other, either in the apprehension or amendment of the wrongs which exist in their necessary relations; but they should harmonize in opinion and co-operate in effort, for the reason that they must unite in the ultimate achievement of the desired reformation.

Of the many points now under discussion, and demanding a just settlement, the general question of woman's rights and relations comprehends these: Her education—literary, scientific, and artistic; her avocations—industrial, commercial, and professional; her interests—pecuniary, civil, and political; in a word, her rights as an individual, and her functions as a citizen.

No one will pretend that all these interests, embracing as they do all that is not merely animal in a human life, are rightly understood, or justly provided for in the existing social order. Nor is it any more true that the constitutional differences of the sexes which should determine, define, and limit the resulting differences of office and duty, are adequately comprehended and practically observed.

Woman has been condemned for her greater delicacy of physical organization, to inferiority of intellectual and moral culture, and to the forfeiture of great social, civil, and religious privileges. In the relation of marriage she has been ideally annihilated and actually enslaved in all that concerns her personal and pecuniary rights, and even in widowed and single life, she is oppressed with such limitation and degradation of labor and avocation, as clearly and cruelly mark the condition of a disabled caste. But by the inspiration of the Almighty, the beneficent spirit of reform is roused to the redress of these wrongs.

The tyranny which degrades and crushes wives and mothers sits no longer lightly on the world's conscience; the heart's home-worship feels the stain of stooping at a dishonored altar. Manhood begins to feel the shame of muddying the springs from which it draws its highest life, and womanhood is everywhere awakening to assert its divinely chartered rights and to fulfill its noblest duties. It is the spirit of reviving truth and righteousness which has moved upon the great deep of the public heart and aroused its redressing justice, and through it the Providence of God is vindicating the order and appointments of His creation.

The signs are encouraging; the time is opportune. Come, then, to this Convention. It is your duty, if you are worthy of your age and country. Give the help of your best thought to separate the light from the darkness. Wisely give the protection of your name, and the benefit of your efforts to the great work of settling the principles, devising the methods, and achieving the success of this high and holy movement.

*   *   *

On the opening day of this second women's rights convention at Worcester, the abolitionist Wendell Phillips delivered the following address. Phillips, a close friend of the radical abolitionist William Lloyd Garrison since the 1830s, was a well-known orator in reform circles. In this speech his radicalism carries over to his views of women's rights. Woman's place, Phillips argues, is not in the home, but in the professions, in politics, even in the military. In time, he says, there could be "a woman Charlemagne, or a Napoleon," but even if future centuries should prove that women have different intellectual abilities from men, they are entitled to equal rights.

WENDELL PHILLIPS TO THE CONVENTION
AT WORCESTER, MASSACHUSETTS,
OCTOBER 15–16, 1851

In drawing up some of these resolutions, I have used very freely the language of a thoughtful and profound article in the *Westminster Review*. It is a review of the proceedings of our Convention, held one year ago, and states with singular clearness and force the leading arguments for our reform, and the grounds of our claim in behalf of woman. I rejoice to see so large an audience gathered to consider this momentous subject, the most magnificent reform that has yet been launched upon the world. It is the first organized protest against the injustice which has brooded over the character and the destiny of one-half of the human race. Nowhere else, under any circumstances, has a demand ever yet been made for the liberties of one whole half of our race. It is fitting that we should pause and consider so remarkable and significant a circumstance; that we should discuss the questions involved with the seriousness and deliberation suitable to such an enterprise.

It strikes, indeed, a great and vital blow at the whole social fabric of every nation; but this, to my mind, is no argument, against it.... Government commenced in usurpation and oppression; liberty and civilization at present are nothing else than the fragments of rights which the scaffold and the stake have wrung from the strong hands of the usurpers. Every step of progress the world has made has been from scaffold to scaffold, from stake to stake.... Government began in tyranny and force; began in the feudalism of the soldier and the bigotry of the priest; and the ideas of justice and humanity have been fighting their way like a thunderstorm against the organized selfishness of human nature.

And this is the last great protest against the wrong of ages. It is no argument, to my mind, therefore, that the old social fabric of the past is against us. Neither do I feel called upon to show what woman's proper sphere is. In every great reform the

---

Source: Elizabeth Cady Stanton, Susan B. Anthony et al., *The History of Woman Suffrage* (6 vols.; New York, 1881–1922; reprint, New York, 1969), vol. 1.

majority have always said to the claimant, no matter what he claimed, "You are not fit for such a privilege." Luther asked of the Pope liberty for the masses to read the Bible. The reply was that it would not be safe to trust the masses with the word of God. "Let them try," said the great reformer, and the history of three centuries of development and purity proclaims the result.

The lower classes in France claimed their civil rights; the right to vote, and to a direct representation in government, but the rich and lettered classes cried out, "You can not be made fit." The answer was, "Let us try." That France is not as Spain, utterly crushed beneath the weight of a thousand years of mis-government, is the answer to those who doubt the ultimate success of the experiment.

Woman stands now at the same door. She says: "You tell me I have no intellect. Give me a chance." "You tell me I shall only embarass politics; let me try." The only reply is the same stale argument that said to the Jews of Europe: You are fit only to make money; you are not fit for the ranks of the army, or the halls of Parliament.

How cogent the eloquent appeal of Macaulay: "What right have we to take this question for granted? Throw open the doors of this House of Commons; throw open the ranks of the imperial army, before you deny eloquence to the countrymen of Isaiah, or valor to the descendants of the Maccabees."

It is the same now with us. Throw open the doors of Congress; throw open those court-houses; throw wide open the doors of your colleges, and give to the sisters of the De Staëls and the Martineaus the same opportunity for culture that men have, and let the results prove what their capacity and intellect really are. When woman has enjoyed for as many centuries as we have the aid of books, the discipline of life, and the stimulus of fame, it will be time to begin the discussion of these questions: "What is the intellect of woman?" "Is it equal to that of man?" Till then, all such discussion is mere beating of the air. While it is doubtless true, that great minds make a way for themselves, spite of all obstacles, yet who knows how many Miltons have died, "mute and inglorious"? However splendid the natural endowments, the discipline of life, after all, completes the miracle. The ability of Napoleon—what was it?

It grew out of the hope to be Cæsar, or Marlborough; out of Austerlitz and Jena—out of his battle-fields, his throne, and all the great scenes of that eventful life.

Open to woman the same scenes, immerse her in the same great interests and pursuits, and if twenty centuries shall not produce a woman Charlemagne, or a Napoleon, fair reason will then allow us to conclude that there is some distinctive peculiarity in the intellects of the sexes.

Centuries alone can lay a fair basis for the argument. I believe on this point there is a shrinking consciousness of not being ready for the battle, on the part of some of the stronger sex, as they call themselves; a tacit confession of risk to this imagined superiority, if they consent to meet their sisters in the lecture halls, or the laboratory of science.

My proof of it is this, that the mightiest intellects of the race, from Plato down to the present time, some of the rarest minds of Germany, France, and England, have successively yielded their assent to the fact, that woman is not, perhaps, identically, but equally endowed with man in all intellectual capabilities. It is generally the second-rate men who doubt; doubt because, perhaps, they fear a fair field.

Suppose that woman is essentially inferior to man, she still has rights. Grant that Mrs. Norton never could be Byron; that Elizabeth Barrett never could have written Paradise Lost; that Mrs. Somerville never could be La Place, nor Sirani have painted the Transfiguration. What then? Does that prove they should be deprived of all civil rights?

John Smith will never be, never can be, Daniel Webster. Shall he therefore be put under guardianship, and forbidden to vote? Suppose woman, though equal, does differ essentially in her intellect from man, is that any ground for disfranchising her? Shall the Fultons say to the Raphaels, because you can not make steam engines, therefore you shall not vote? Shall the

---

Note: Caroline Norton was an English author. Elizabeth Barrett was an English poet (better known as Elizabeth Barrett Browning). John Smith, however, was not the Virginia colonist, but merely a name, like "John Doe" for the ordinary man. Daniel Webster, the famous lawyer/politician/orator, then secretary of state, was especially well known in his home state of Massachusetts.

Napoleons or the Washingtons say to the Wordsworths or the Herschels, because you can not lead armies, and govern States, therefore you shall have no civil rights?

*   *   *

LETTER OF HARRIET MARTINEAU, 1851

A letter the English author Harriet Martineau had written to Paulina Wright Davis, the president of the Worcester Convention, was read at the 1851 meeting. Martineau thanks Davis for having sent her the previous year's convention account, and then launches into her own views of women's equality. She dismisses arguments over "womans' sphere" as "mere beating of the air." But, like several other women's rights advocates, she points out the untried nature of women's intellectual abilities.

CROMER, ENGLAND, Aug. 3, 1851.

DEAR MADAM:—I beg to thank you heartily for your kindness in sending me the Report of the Proceedings of your Woman's Rights Convention. I had gathered what I could from the newspapers concerning it, but I was gratified at being able to read, in a collected form, addresses so full of earnestness and sound truth, as I found most of the speeches to be. I hope you are aware of the interest excited in this country by that Convention, the strongest proof of which is the appearance of an article on the subject in *The Westminster Review* (for July), as thorough-going as any of your own addresses, and from the pen (at least as it is understood here) of one of our very first men, Mr. John S. Mill. I am not without hope that this article will materially strengthen your hands, and I am sure it can not but cheer your hearts.

Ever since I became capable of thinking for myself, I have clearly seen, and I have said it till my listeners and readers are probably tired of hearing it, that there can be but one true method in the treatment of each human being, of either sex, of any color, and under any outward circumstances, to ascertain what are the powers of that being, to cultivate them to the utmost, and *then* to see what action they will find for themselves. This has probably never been done for men, unless in some rare individual cases. It has certainly never been done for women, and, till it is done, all debating about what woman's intellect is, all speculation, or laying down the law, as to what is woman's sphere, is a mere beating of the air. *A priori* conceptions have long been worthless in physical science, and nothing was really effected till the experimental method was clearly made out and strictly applied in practice, and the same principle holds most certainly through the whole range of moral science.

Whether we regard the physical fact of what women are able to do, or the moral fact of what women ought to do, it is equally necessary to abstain from making any decision prior to experiment. We see plainly enough the waste of time and thought among the men who once talked of Nature abhorring a vacuum, or disputed at great length as to whether angels could go from end to end without passing through the middle; and the day will come when it will appear to be no less absurd to have argued, as men and women are arguing now, about what woman ought to do, before it was ascertained what woman can do.

Let us once see a hundred women educated up to the highest point that education at present reaches; let them be supplied with such knowledge as their faculties are found to crave, and let them be free to use, apply, and increase their knowledge as their faculties shall instigate, and it will presently appear what is the sphere of each of the hundred.

One may be discovering comets, like Miss Herschel; one may be laying open the mathematical structure of the universe, like Mrs. Somerville; another may be analyzing the chemical relations of Nature in the laboratory; another may be penetrating the mysteries of physiology; others may be applying science in the healing of diseases; others may be investigating the laws of social relations, learning the great natural laws under which society, like everything else, proceeds; others, again, may be actively carrying out the social arrangements which have been formed under these laws; and others may be chiefly occupied in family business, in the duties of the wife and mother, and the ruler of the household.

If, among the hundred women, a great diversity of powers should appear (which I have no doubt would be the case), there will always be plenty of scope and material for the greatest amount and variety of power that can be brought out. If not— if it should appear that women fall below men in all but the domestic functions—then it will be well that the experiment has been tried; and the trial better go on forever, that woman's sphere may forever determine itself to the satisfaction of everybody. It is clear that education, to be what I demand on behalf of women, must be intended to issue in active life.

A man's medical education would be worth little, if it was not a preparation for practice. The astronomer and the chemist would put little force into their studies, if it was certain that they must leave off in four or five years, and do nothing for the rest of their lives; and no man could possibly feel much interest in political and social morals, if he knew that he must, all his life long, pay taxes, but neither speak nor move about public affairs.

Women, like men, must be educated with a view to action, or their studies can not be called education, and no judgment can be formed of the scope of their faculties. The pursuit must be life's business, or it will be mere pastime or irksome task. This was always my point of difference with one who carefully cherished a reverence for woman, the late Dr. Channing.

How much we spoke and wrote of the old controversy, Influence *vs.* Office. He would have had any woman study anything that her faculties led her to, whether physical science or law, government and political economy; but he would have her stop at the study. From the moment she entered the hospital as physician and not nurse; from the moment she took her place in a court of justice, in the jury box, and not the witness box; from the moment she brought her mind and her voice into the legislature, instead of discussing the principles of laws at home; from the moment she announced and administered justice instead of looking at it from afar, as a thing with which she had no concern, she would, he feared, lose her influence as an observing intelligence, standing by in a state of purity "unspotted from the world."

My conviction always was, that an intelligence never carried out into action could not be worth much; and that, if all the action of human life was of a character so tainted as to be unfit for women, it could be no better for men, and we ought all to sit down together, to let barbarism overtake us once more.

My own conviction is, that the natural action of the whole human being occasions not only the most strength, but the highest elevation; not only the warmest sympathy, but the deepest purity. The highest and purest beings among women seem now to be those who, far from being idle, find among their restricted opportunities some means of strenuous action; and I can not doubt that, if an active social career were open to all women, with due means of preparation for it, those who are high and holy now, would be high and holy then, and would be joined by an innumerable company of just spirits from among those whose energies are now pining and fretting in enforced idleness, or unworthy frivolity, or brought down into pursuits and aims which are anything but pure and peaceable.

In regard to the old controversy—Influence *vs.* Office—it appears to me that if Influence is good and Office bad for human morals and character, Man's present position is one of such hardship, as it is almost profane to contemplate; and if, on the contrary, Office is good and a life of Influence is bad, Woman has an instant right to claim that her position be amended.

Yours faithfully,

HARRIET MARTINEAU.

Akron, Ohio, 1851

Frances D. Gage, a wife, mother, and writer on other reform causes as well as women's rights, was chosen president of the Akron convention on May 28, 1851. Her acceptance speech draws upon the lessons of history, recalling the hardships the early colonists endured in settling the wilderness and comparing their struggle to nineteenth-century women's efforts to overcome "a wilderness of prejudice" in securing their rights.

ADDRESS OF PRESIDENT FRANCES GAGE

I am at a loss, kind friends, to know whether to return you thanks, or not, for the honor conferred upon me. And when I tell you that I have never in my life attended a regular business meeting, and am entirely inexperienced in the forms and ceremonies of a deliberative body, you will not be surprised that I do not feel remarkably grateful for the position. For though you have conferred an honor upon me, I very much fear I shall not be able to reflect it back. I will try.

When our forefathers left the old and beaten paths of New England, and struck out for themselves in a new and unexplored country, they went forth with a slow and cautious step, but with firm and resolute hearts. The land of their fathers had become too small for their children. Its soil answered not their wants. The parents shook their heads and said, with doubtful and foreboding faces: "Stand still, stay at home. This has sufficed for us;

Source: Elizabeth Cady Stanton, Susan B. Anthony et al., *The History of Woman Suffrage* (6 vols.; New York, 1881–1922; reprint, New York, 1969), vol. 1.

we have lived and enjoyed ourselves here. True, our mountains are high and our soil is rugged and cold; but you won't find a better; change, and trial, and toil, will meet you at every step. Stay, tarry with us, and go not forth to the wilderness."

But the children answered: "Let us go; this land has sufficed for you, but the one beyond the mountains is better. We know there is trial, toil, and danger; but for the sake of our children, and our children's children, we are willing to meet all." They went forth, and pitched their tents in the wilderness. An herculean task was before them; the rich and fertile soil was shadowed by a mighty forest, and giant trees were to be felled. The Indians roamed the wild, wide hunting-grounds, and claimed them as their own. They must be met and subdued. The savage beasts howled defiance from every hill-top, and in every glen. They must be destroyed. Did the hearts of our fathers fail? No; they entered upon their new life, their new world, with a strong faith and a mighty will. For they saw in the prospection a great and incalculable good. It was not the work of an hour, nor of a day; not of weeks or months, but of long struggling, toiling, painful years. If they failed at one point, they took hold of another. If their paths through the wilderness were at first crooked, rough, and dangerous, by little and little they improved them. The forest faded away, the savage disappeared, the wild beasts were destroyed, and the hopes and prophetic visions of their far-seeing powers in the new and untried country, were more than realized.

Permit me to draw a comparison between the situation of our forefathers in the wilderness, without even so much as a bridle-path through its dark depths, and our present position. The old land of moral, social, and political privilege, seems too narrow for our wants; its soil answers not to our growing, and we feel that we see clearly a better country that we might inhabit. But there are mountains of established law and custom to overcome; a wilderness of prejudice to be subdued; a powerful foe of selfishness and self-interest to overthrow; wild beasts of pride, envy, malice, and hate to destroy. But for the sake of our children and our children's children, we have entered upon the work, hoping and praying that we may be guided by wisdom, sustained by love, and led and cheered by the earnest hope of doing good.

I shall enter into no labored argument to prove that woman does not occupy the position in society to which her capacity justly entitles her. The rights of mankind emanate from their natural wants and emotions. Are not the natural wants and emotions of humanity common to, and shared equally by, both sexes? Does man hunger and thirst, suffer cold and heat more than woman? Does he love and hate, hope and fear, joy and sorrow more than woman? Does his heart thrill with a deeper pleasure in doing good? Can his soul writhe in more bitter agony under the consciousness of evil or wrong? Is the sunshine more glorious, the air more quiet, the sounds of harmony more soothing, the perfume of flowers more exquisite, or forms of beauty more soul-satisfying to his senses, than to hers? To all these interrogatories every one will answer, No!

Where then did man get the authority that he now claims over one-half of humanity? From what power the vested right to place woman—his partner, his companion, his helpmeet in life—in an inferior position? Came it from nature? Nature made woman his superior when she made her his mother; his equal when she fitted her to hold the sacred position of wife. Does he draw his authority from God, from the language of holy writ? No! For it says that "Male and female created he *them*, and gave *them* dominion." Does he claim it under law of the land? Did woman meet with him in council and voluntarily give up all her claim to be her own law-maker? Or did the majesty of might place this power in his hands?—The power of the strong over the weak makes man the master! Yes, there, and there only, does he gain his authority.

In the dark ages of the past, when ignorance, superstition, and bigotry held rule in the world, might made the law. But the undertone, the still small voices of Justice, Love, and Mercy, have ever been heard, pleading the cause of humanity, pleading for truth and right; and their low, soft tones of harmony have softened the lion heart of might, and, little by little, he has yielded as the centuries rolled on; and man, as well as woman, has been the gainer by every concession. We will ask him to yield still; to allow the voice of woman to be heard; to let her take the position which her wants and emotions seem to require; to let her enjoy her natural rights. Do not answer that woman's position is now all her natural wants and emotions require. Our meeting here together this day proves the contrary; proves that we have aspirations that are not met. Will it be answered that we are factious, discontented spirits, striving to disturb the public order, and tear up the old fastnesses of society? So it was said of Jesus Christ and His followers, when they taught peace on earth and good-will to men. So it was said of our forefathers in the great struggle for freedom. So it has been said of every reformer that has ever started out the car of progress on a new and untried track.

We fear not man as an enemy. He is our friend, our brother. Let woman speak for herself, and she will be heard. Let her claim with a calm and determined, yet loving spirit, her place, and it will be given her. I pour out no harsh invectives against the present order of things—against our fathers, husbands, and brothers; they do as they have been taught; they feel as society bids them; they act as the law requires. Woman must act for herself.

Oh, if all women could be impressed with the importance of their own action, and with one united voice, speak out in their own behalf, in behalf of humanity, they could create a revolution without armies, without bloodshed, that would do more to ameliorate the condition of mankind, to purify, elevate, ennoble humanity, than all that has been done by reformers in the last century.

*   *   *

SOJOURNER TRUTH'S SPEECH, 1851

Another woman's rights advocate would become widely known for a single speech delivered in Ohio in the summer of 1851. Sojourner Truth, who was born a slave named Isabella, by the 1840s had renamed herself and dedicated her life to traveling through New York and New England and speaking to abolitionist and religious audiences. Over six feet tall, very dark-skinned, and striking in appearance, the illiterate ex-slave was an eloquent orator who, as Frederick Douglass once said, "cared very little for elegance of speech or refinement of manners." She spoke at the national women's rights convention at Worcester, Massachusetts, in 1850, and in 1851 she addressed the women's convention in Akron, Ohio. The text of her speech as reported by a local antislavery paper appears below. Years later Frances Dana Gage recalled the power of Sojourner Truth's speech, which included the repetition of one striking question, "Ar'n't I a woman?" as a poignant example of the denial of rights to African American women. Gage set down her recollection of the speech in a letter published in 1863. Recent research suggests that Gage may have embroidered her recollections of Sojourner Truth's speech. On the other hand, is it possible that the reporter of the Salem, Ohio, paper left out the emotional question and merely reconstructed a brief version of the speech?

SOJOURNER TRUTH'S SPEECH
(As reported in the *Anti-Slavery Bugle*, June 21, 1851)

One of the most unique and interesting speeches of the Convention was made by Sojourner Truth, an emancipated slave. It is impossible to transfer it to paper, or convey any adequate idea of the effect it produced upon the audience. Those only can appreciate it who saw her powerful form, her whole-souled, earnest gestures, and listened to her strong and truthful tones. She came forward to the platform and addressing the President said with great simplicity:

May I say a few words? Receiving an affirmative answer, she proceeded; I want to say a few words about this matter. I am a woman's rights [*sic*]. I have as much muscle as any man, and can do as much work as any man. I have plowed and reaped and husked and chopped and mowed, and can any man

---

Source: The *Anti-Slavery Bugle* (Salem, Ohio), 21 June, 1851.

do more than that? I have heard much about the sexes being equal; I can carry as much as any man, and can eat as much too, if I can get it. I am as strong as any man that is now. As for intellect, all I can say is, if a woman have a pint and a man a quart—why cant she have her little pint full? You need not be afraid to give us our rights for fear we will take too much,— for we can't take more than our pint'll hold. The poor men seem to be all in confusion, and don't know what to do. Why children, if you have woman's rights give it to her and you will feel better. You will have your own rights, and they wont be so much trouble. I can't read, but I can hear. I have heard the bible and have learned that Eve caused man to sin. Well if woman upset the world, do give her a chance to set it right side up again. The lady has spoken about Jesus, how he never spurned woman from him, and she was right. When Lazarus died, Mary and Martha came to him with faith and love and besought him to raise their brother. And Jesus wept—and Lazarus came forth. And how came Jesus into the world? Through God who created him and woman who bore him. Man, where is your part? But the women are coming up blessed be God and a few of the men are coming up with them. But man is in a tight place, the poor slave is on him, woman is coming on him, and he is surely between a hawk and a buzzard.

*   *   *

SOJOURNER TRUTH'S "AR'N'T I A WOMAN?" SPEECH
(As recalled by Frances Dana Gage in 1863)

. . . In the spring of 1851, a Woman's Rights Convention was called in Akron, Ohio, by the friends of that then wondrously unpopular cause. I attended that Convention. No one at this day can conceive of the state of feeling of the multitude that came together on that occasion.

Source: The *Independent,* April 23, 1863.

The Convention in the spring of 1850, in Salem, Ohio, reported at length in *The New York Tribune* by that staunch friend of Human rights, Oliver Johnson, followed in October of the same year by another convention at Worcester, Mass., well reported and well abused, with divers minor conventions, each amply vilified and caricatured, had set the world all agog, and the people, finding the women *in earnest,* turned out in large numbers to see and hear.

The leaders of the movement, staggering under the weight of disapprobation already laid upon them, and tremblingly alive to every appearance of evil that might spring up in their midst, were many of them almost thrown into panics on the first day of the meeting, by seeing a tall, gaunt black woman in a gray dress and white turban, surmounted by an uncouth sun-bonnet, march deliberately into the church, walk with the air of a queen up the aisle, and take her seat upon the pulpit steps. A buzz of disapprobation was heard all over the house, and such words as these fell upon listening ears:

"An abolition affair!" "Women's Rights and niggers!" "We told you so. Go it, old darky!"

I chanced upon that occasion to wear my first laurels in public life, as president of the meeting. At my request, order was restored, and the business of the hour went on. The morning session closed; the afternoon session was held; the evening exercises came and went; old Sojourner, quiet and reticent as the "Libyan Statue," sat crouched against the wall on a corner of the pulpit stairs, her sun-bonnet shading her eyes, her elbow on her knee, and her chin resting on her broad, hard palm.

At intermissions she was busy selling the "Life of Sojourner Truth," a narrative of her own strange and adventurous life.

Again and again timorous and trembling ones came to me and said with earnestness, "Don't let her speak, Mrs. G. It will ruin us. Every newspaper in the land will have our cause mixed with abolition and niggers, and we shall be utterly denounced." My only answer was, "We shall see when the time comes."

The second day the work waxed warm. Methodist, Baptist,

Sojourner Truth. In her bag she often carried copies of the narrative of her life to sell. *(Courtesy: State University College, New Paltz, N.Y.)*

Episcopal, Presbyterian, and Universalist ministers came in to hear and discuss the resolutions brought forth. One claimed superior rights and privileges for man because of superior intellect; another because of the manhood of Christ. If God had desired the equality of woman, he would have given some token of his will through the birth, life, and death of the Savior. Another gave us a theological view of the awful sin of our first mother. There were few women in those days that dared to "speak in meeting," and the august teachers of the people, with long-winded bombast, were seeming to get the better of us, while the boys in the galleries and sneerers among the pews were enjoying hugely the discomfiture, as they supposed, of the strong-minded. Some of the tender-skinned friends were growing indignant and on the point of losing dignity, and the atmosphere of the convention betokened a storm.

Slowly from her seat in the corner rose Sojourner Truth, who, till now, had hardly lifted her head. "Don't let her speak," gasped a half-dozen in my ear. She moved slowly and solemnly to the front; laid her old bonnet at her feet, and turned her great speaking eyes to me.

There was a hissing sound of disapprobation above and below. I rose and announced "Sojourner Truth," and begged the audience to keep silence for a few moments. The tumult subsided at once, and every eye was fixed on this almost Amazon form, which stood nearly six feet high, head erect, an eye piercing the upper air like one in a dream. At her first word there was a profound hush. She spoke in deep tones, which, though not loud, reached every ear in the house, and away through the throng at the doors and windows.

"Well, chillen, whar dar's so much racket dar must be som'ting out o'kilter. I tink dat, 'twixt the niggers of de Souf and de women at de Norf, all a-talking 'bout rights, de white men will be in a fix pretty soon. But what's all this here talking 'bout? Dat man over dar say dat woman needs to be helped into carriages, and lifted ober ditches, and to have de best place eberywhar. Nobody eber helps me into carriages, or ober mud-puddles, or gives me any best place;" and, raising herself to her full height, and her voice to a pitch like rolling thunder, she asked, "And ar'n't I a woman? Look at me. Look at my arm," and she bared her right arm to the shoulder, showing its tremendous muscular power. "I have plowed and planted and gathered into barns, and no man could head me—and ar'n't I a woman? I could work as much and eat as much as a man, (when I could get it,) and bear de lash as well—and ar'n't I a woman? I have borne thirteen chillen, and seen 'em mos' all sold off into slavery, and when I cried out with a mother's grief, none but Jesus heard—and ar'n't I a woman? When dey talks 'bout dis ting in de head. What dis dey call it?" "Intellect," whispered some one near. "Dat's it, honey. What's dat got to do with woman's rights or nigger's rights? If my cup won't hold but a pint and yourn holds a quart, wouldn't ye be mean not to let me have my little half-measure full?" and she pointed her significant finger and sent a keen glance at the minister who had made the argument. The cheering was long and loud. "Den dat little man in black dar, he say woman can't have as much right as man 'cause Christ wa'n't a woman. *Whar did your Christ come from?"*

Rolling thunder could not have stilled that crowd as did those deep wonderful tones, as she stood there with outstretched arms and eye of fire. Raising her voice still louder, she repeated,

"Whar did your Christ come from? From God and a woman. Man had noting to do with him." Oh! what a rebuke she gave the little man. Turning again to another objector, she took up the defense of Mother Eve. I cannot follow her through it all. It was pointed and witty and solemn; eliciting at almost every sentence deafening applause; and she ended by asserting "that if de fust woman God ever made was strong enough to turn de world upside down all her one lone, all dese togeder," and she glanced her eye over us, "ought to be able to turn it back an git it right side up again, and now dey is asking to, de men better let 'em." (Long continuous cheering.) " 'Bleeged to ye for hearin' on me, and now old Sojourner ha'n't got nothin' more to say."

Amid roars of applause she turned to her corner, leaving more than one of us with streaming eyes and hearts beating with gratitude. She had taken us up in her great strong arms and carried us safely over the slough of difficulty, turning the whole tide in our favor.

I have given but a faint sketch of her speech. I have never in my life seen anything like the magical influence that subdued the mobbish spirit of the day, and turned the jibes and sneers of an excited crowd into notes of respect and admiration. Hundreds rushed up to shake hands and congratulate the glorious old mother, and bid her "God-speed" on her mission of "testifying agin concernin' the wickedness of this here people."

Once upon a Sabbath in Michigan an abolition meeting was held. Parker Pillsbury was speaker, and expressed himself freely upon the conduct of the churches regarding slavery. While he spoke, there came up a fearful thunder-storm. A young Methodist rose and, interrupting him, said he felt alarmed; he felt as if God's judgment was about to fall upon him for daring to sit and hear such blasphemy; that it made his hair almost rise with terror. Here a voice sounding above the rain that beat upon the roof, the sweeping surge of the winds, the crashing of the limbs of trees, swaying of branches, and the rolling of thunder, spoke out: "Chile, don't be skeered; you're not goin' to be harmed. I don't speck God's ever heern tell on ye!"

It was all she said, but it was enough. I might multiply anecdotes (and some of the best cannot be told) till your pages would not contain them, and yet the fund not be exhausted. Therefore, I will close, only saying to those who think public opinion does not change, that they have only to look at the progress of ideas from the standpoint of old Sojourner Truth twelve years ago. . . .

Westchester, Pennsylvania, 1852

Ann Preston's "Address"

The following address, written by Miss Ann Preston, and designed for adoption by the Convention as an exposition of its principles and purposes, was impressively read by the author at the Woman's Rights Convention at Westchester, Pa.

ADDRESS.

The question is repeatedly asked by those who have thought but little upon the subject of woman's position in society, "What does woman want more than she possesses already? Is she not beloved, honored, guarded, cherished?—Wherein are her rights infringed, or her liberties curtailed?"

Glowing pictures have been drawn of the fitness of the present relations of society, and of the beauty of woman's dependence upon the protecting love of man; and frightful visions have been evoked of the confusion and perversion of nature which would occur if the doctrine of the equal rights of man and woman was once admitted.

The idea seems to prevail that movements for the elevation of woman arise not from the legitimate wants of society, but from the vague restlessness of unquiet spirits; not from the serene dictates of wisdom, but from the headlong impulses of fanaticism.

We came not here to argue the question of the relative strength of intellect in man and woman, for the reform which we advocate depends not upon its settlement.

Source: Ann Preston, "Address," *The Lily* 4, no. 8 (Aug. 1852).

We place not the interests of woman in antagonism to that of her brother, for

> "The woman's cause is man's.
>   They rise or sink together,
>   Dwarfed or God-like, bond or free."

We maintain not that woman should lose any of that refinement and delicacy of spirit which, as a celestial halo, ever encircles the pure in heart.

We contend not that she shall become noisy and dictatorial, and abjure the quiet graces of life.

We claim not that she, any more than her mother, should engage in any occupation, or appear in any situation to which her nature and abilities are not fitted.

But we ask for her, as for man, equality before the law, and freedom to exercise all her powers and faculties under the direction of her own judgment and volition.

When a woman dies leaving behind her a husband and children, no appraisers come into the desolated home to examine the effects; the father is the guardian of his offspring; the family relation is not invaded by law. But when a man dies, the case is entirely different; in the hour of the widow's desolation, strangers come into the house to take an inventory of the effects, strangers are appointed to be the guardians of her children, and she, their natural caretaker, thenceforth has no legal direction of their interests; strangers decide upon the propriety of the sale of the property—earned, perhaps, by her own and her husband's mutual efforts—and her interest in the estate is coolly designated as the *"widow's encumbrance!"*

In the extremity of her bereavement, there is piled upon her, not only the dread of separation from her children, but that of being sent homeless from the spot where every object has been consecrated by her tenderest affections.

Nor is the practical working of this law better than its theory; all over the country there are widows who have been made doubly desolate by its provisions—widows separated from their children, who, if they had had the disposal of their own and their husband's mutual property, might have retrieved their circumstances, and kept the household band together.

We ask for such change in public sentiment as shall procure the repeal of this oppressive law.

We ask that woman shall have free access to vocations of profit and honor, the means of earning a livelihood and independence for herself! As a general rule, profitable employments are not considered open to woman, nor are her business capabilities encouraged and developed by systematic training. Gloomy must be the feelings of the father of a family of young daughters when he is about to bid farewell to the world, if he is leaving them without the means of pecuniary support. Their brothers may go out into society and gain position and competency; but for them there is but little choice of employment, and, too often, they are left with depressed and crippled energies to pine and chafe under the bitter sense of poverty and dependence.

Their pursuits are to be determined, not by their inclination, judgment, and ability, as are those of man, but by the popular estimate of what is proper and becoming. In Turkey, public delicacy is outraged if a woman appears unveiled beyond the walls of the Harem; in America a sentiment no less arbitrary presumes to chalk out for her the precise boundaries of womanly propriety; and she who ventures to step beyond them, must do it at the peril of encountering low sneers, coarse allusions, and the withering imputation of want of feminine delicacy.

Even for the same services woman generally receives less than man. The whole tendency of our customs, habits and teaching, is to make her *dependent*—dependent in outward circumstances, dependent in spirit.

As a consequence of her fewer resources, marriage has been to her the great means of securing position in society. Thus it is that this relation, which should ever be a "holy sacrament"—the unbiased and generous election of the free and self-sustained being, too often is degraded into a mean acceptance of a shelter from neglect and poverty!

We ask that woman shall be trained to unfold her whole nature, to exercise all her powers and faculties.

It is said that the domestic circle is the peculiar province of woman; that "men are what mothers make them." But how can that woman who does not live for self-culture and self-development, who has herself no exalted objects in life, imbue her children with lofty aspirations, or train her sons to a free and glorious manhood?

She best can fulfill the duties of wife and mother, who is fitted for other and varied usefulness.

The being who lives for one relation only, cannot possess the power and scope which are required for the highest excellence even in that one. If the whole body is left without exercise, one arm does not become strong; if the tree is stunted in its growth, one branch does not shoot into surpassing luxuriance.

That woman whose habits and mental training enable her to assist and sustain her husband in seasons of difficulty, and whose children rely on her as a wise counsellor,—commands a life-long reverence far deeper and dearer than can be secured by transient accomplishments, of the most refined and delicate imbecility.

All women are not wives and mothers, but all have spirits needing development—powers that grow with their exercise.

Those who are best acquainted with the state of society know that there is, at this time, a vast amount of unhappiness among women for want of free outlets to their powers; that thousands are yearning for fuller development, and a wider field of usefulness. The same energies which in man find vent in professions, and in the thousand forms of business and study, must find an ennobling channel in woman, else they will be frittered away in trifles, or turned into instruments to prey upon their possessor.

To follow the empty round of fashion, to retail gossip and scandal, to be an ornament in the parlor or a mere drudge in the kitchen, to live as an appendage to any human being, does not fill up nor satisfy the capacities of a soul awakened to a sense of its true wants, and of the far-reaching and mighty interests which cluster around its existence.

We protest against the tyranny of that public sentiment which assigns any arbitrary sphere to woman.

God has made the happiness and development of His creatures to depend upon the free exercise of their powers and faculties. Freedom is the law of beauty, written by His fingers upon the human mind, and the only condition upon which it can attain to its full stature, and expand in its natural and beautiful preparations.

It is recognized, in reference to man, that his judgment, opportunities and abilities are the only proper measure of his sphere. "The tools to him who can use them." But the same principles are not trusted in their application to woman, less, forsooth, she should lose her feminine characteristics, and like the lost pleaid forsake her native sphere!

It seems to be forgotten that the laws of nature will not be suspended; that the human mind, when released from pressure, like water, must find its own level; that woman cannot, if she would, cast away her nature and instincts; that it is only when we are left free to observe the inward attractions of our being, that we fall into our natural place, and move in our God-appointed orbits.

We ask that none shall dare to come in between woman and her Maker, and with unhallowed hands attempt to plant their shallow posts and draw their flimsy cords around the Heaven-wide spherc of an immortal spirit!

We maintain that God has not so failed in his adaptations as to give powers to be wasted, talents to be wrapped in a napkin, and that the possession of faculties and capabilities is the warrant of nature, the command of the All-Wise for their culture and exercise.

We believe that the woman who is obeying the convictions of her own soul, and whose ability is commensurate with her employment, is ever in her own true sphere, whether in her quiet home she is training her children to nobleness and virtue, or is standing as a physician by the bed of sickness and sorrow. . . .

While we demand for woman a more complete physical, intellectual and moral education, as the means of strengthening and beautifying her own nature, and of ennobling the whole race, we also ask for a more elevated standard of excellence and moral purity in *man:* and we maintain that if there is any place of resort, or any employment in society, which, *necessarily*, would sully the delicacy of woman's spirit, in that man also must be contaminated and degraded.

Woman indeed should wear about her, wherever she moves, the protecting investment of innocence and purity, but not less is it requisite that he, who is the companion of her life, should guard his spirit with the same sacred and beautiful covering.

We believe that woman, as an accountable being, cannot innocently merge her individuality in that of her brother or accept from him the limitation of her sphere.

In all life's great extremities she also is thrown upon her inward resources, and stands alone.—Man cannot step in between her and the "accusing angel" of her own conscience; alone in the solitude of her spirit she must wrestle with her own sorrows; none can walk for her "the valley of the shadow of death!" When her brother shall be able to settle for her accountabilities, and "give to God a ransom for her soul," then, and not till then, may she rightly commit to him the direction of her powers and activities.

We ask, in fine, for the application of the fundamental principles of Christianity and republicanism to this, as to all other questions of vital importance; and appealing to all who desire the progression and happiness of the whole race, we ask them, as magnanimous men and true women, to examine this subject in the spirit of a generous and candid investigation.

"National Woman's Rights Convention"

THE LILY, October 1852

This Convention assembled pursuant to the call of the Central Committee at Syracuse, on Wednesday, the 8th of September, and continued in session three days. In our limited space it is entirely impossible for us to give a full report of the proceedings, but shall endeavor to present a brief sketch of the more important matters brought before it.

The following were the officers of the Convention:

President—Mrs. LUCRETIA MOTT.

Vice Presidents—Mrs. PAULINA W. DAVIS of R.I., Mrs. E. OAKES SMITH of N.Y.

Secretaries—Mrs. Clementine Nichols of Vt., Gerrit Smith of N.Y., Mrs. Sarah L. Miller of Penn., Miss Susan B. Anthony, N.Y., Martha C. Wright, Samuel J. May, Mrs. Lydia N. Fowler.

These nominations were confirmed, James Mott only voting in the negative. The gentlemen present cheered the nominations.

Mrs. MOTT then took the chair and addressed the Convention. She had great objections to taking the chair, and the Convention would find out their mistake. She invoked a careful attention to the business of the meeting, and in dispensing with all egotism. She referred also to the favorable success which had attended previous meetings, and alluded to the almost unanimous courtesy of the public journals where their conventions had been held. She wished this meeting to carry out the purpose for which it was called, and to keep up in interest with

Source: "National Woman's Rights Convention," *The Lily* 4, no. 10 (Oct. 1852).

prior conventions. She wished all votes to be given in a firm voice, and speakers first to address the chair, and then turn, facing the audience. The voice could be improved by carefully modulating it.—As to woman's rights, nothing short of universal rights could meet the contingency. (Cheers.)

The Vice Presidents then took seats inside the stand.

Mrs. E. L. ROSE then moved the appointment of a Business Committee, and carried.—Mrs. E. Oakes Smith, Sarah Miller of Penn., Lucy Stone, of Mass., James Mott, of Penn., Mrs. C. M. Severance of Ohio, Ernestine L. Rose, of New York city, Paulina W. Davis, of R.I., Elizabeth W. Phillips, Harriet K. Hunt, of Mass., Pliny Sexton, Elizabeth Jones, Gerrit Smith and Benj. S. Jones, were appointed such Committee.

The following were the principal Resolutions brought before the Convention and adopted:

Proposed by Mrs. E. OAKES SMITH, from the Business Committee:

Inasmuch as many of the institutions handed down to us from the past like heir-looms, are felt to be—though time-honored—hindrances to human progress, and opposed to that Divine Truth which gives light to the world, therefore,

Resolved, That it is our duty to examine these institutions, and ascertain which of them are still worthy of our honor and support—which we should seek to re-form and which to cast aside.

Resolved, That it is the right of every woman holding property, and as a citizen also of the Republic, to resist taxation, till such time as she is fully represented at the Ballot Box.

GERRIT SMITH, from the Business Committee, reported the following resolutions:

Resolved, That the demand of Woman is not for privileges, nor favor, nor employments, nor honors, but for RIGHTS.

Resolved, That the rights of human beings to their own persons, their own earnings and property, and to participate in the choice of the civil rulers, are rights which belong as naturally and absolutely and fully to Woman as to Man.

Resolved, That we beseech Woman never to consent to hold any of these great sacred rights in abeyance; and never to consent to exchange any of them for bribes and privileges, or favors and flatteries, however alluring and seductive.

These resolutions were then accepted.

Mrs. E. OAKES SMITH then proceeded to address the assembly. We have convened to disorganize time-honored institutions. All our heads will be in the grave before these objects are gained. We have not come to speak of private wrongs. Men tell us we are unfit for the position which we seek. Because we have not the heads of gladiators and pugilists, must we be denied the privilege of using what brain we have. Let Syracuse, which has become the Thermopylæ of liberty, be the place for our struggle. (Cheers)

She hoped that this was not a mere talking Convention. We have talked for years. We must now act. She had traveled west, and east, and north, and the friends every where said, "Organize." We want no more Helots; no more judicial murders; no more abandoned outcasts. We must extend our industry into every department and profession, for which we have ability. In spite of St. Paul we must preach.

GERRIT SMITH said that the men had been complained of to-day as taking great liberties with the rights of women. They had been taking as great liberty with his rights. They were determined to have a speech out of him.—He objected to Mr. Neal's compliments to woman, as though she was an angel. She is not an angel! (Cheers.) She is a woman. I do not believe in getting her to heaven before her time. Mr. S. went on to defend the rights of women to vote. He said that he wished women to have a fair field to test their ability. It was time to criticise the experiment when it had been tried. Her rights in every respect were involved in her rights at the Ballot Box.

Miss ANTHONY read an address to the Convention, written by Elizabeth Cady Stanton. The scope of it was the duty of property-holding women to refuse paying taxes, when not represented in Legislative bodies.

Mrs. GAGE offered the following resolution:

Inasmuch as the peace of societies depends on the promotion of justice, and the happiness of mankind on the enjoyment of their rights; and as the absolute rights and natural equality of both sexes are self-evident and cannot be given by favor, but eternally exist, therefore,

Resolved, That it is the imperious obligation of every woman to enter into the discharge of the duties arising from these natural rights to the greatest possible extent; and that we will hereafter direct our strenuous efforts to the acquiring of those rights now forcibly withheld.

Mrs. E. O. SMITH offered the following resolution:

Resolved, That as the imbruted slave who is content with his lot and would not be free if he could, if any such there be, only gives evidence of the depth of his degradation, so the woman who is satisfied with her inferior condition, averring that she has all the rights she wants, does but exhibit the enervating effect of the wrongs to which she is subject.

The resolution offered by Mrs. Gage she advocated in a very able and excellent address.

Miss ANTOINETTE BROWN took up the Bible argument, preceding it with this resolution:

Resolved, That the Bible recognizes the rights, duties, and privileges of Woman as a public teacher, as every way equal with those of man; that it enjoins upon her no subjection that is not enjoined upon him; and that it truly and practically recognizes neither male and female in Christ Jesus.

Miss Brown in the course of her speech in support of this resolution, which was adopted, said:

The passage quoted, "Thy desire shall be thy husband and he shall rule over thee," is based as the reason of her subjection. This she contended meant a prediction, not a command. When Paul says "wives be subject to your husbands," it is in connection with a similar injunction, "Yea, all of you be subject to one another." Paul had many women as fellow helpers. Man we grant is the "head of the woman." This does not mean power, authority, or giving laws, but simply preeminence. Man is the head of woman as Christ is the head of the Church. This means oneness, co-heirship. She cited, "I suffer not women to speak in the churches." The speaking meant as much singing as talking—it was using the voice. But Paul was only forbidding her to interrupt proceedings in the church; not silence but order. He would also have given men the same command. Women had prophesied from the earliest Bible times. Out of the abundance of her heart, woman will teach—they are one in Christ Jesus.

Mrs. NICHOLS, of Vt. presented the following resolution:

Resolved, That equally involved as they are by the ordinance of God, in the natural relations which lie at the base of all Society, the sexes are equally entitled by original claim to all the rights which cover *means* for the discharge of the responsibilities involved in those relations.

Mrs. NICHOLS took the stand to define her position, politically, as Editor of a political newspaper. It had been reported that her paper supported Pierce and King. This she denied. She could not belie her Democratic principles by supporting a pro-Slavery candidate. She then spoke of her property relations, evincing great acquaintance with the structure of the law's relations.—She made several strong points—answered the objection that women were feeble, comparatively, and could not earn so much, therefore they should not have an equal voice. She asked which was worth the most, the children which the woman bore, and nursed, and trained, or the bread and butter which the husband earned?

ABBY H. PRICE, of Hopedale, offered an address based upon Woman's position in the Church.

The Convention was addressed by Mrs. PAULINA W. DAVIS, in a speech of great beauty of diction and importance of matter—referring to the social relations of Woman, particularly to marriage—at the conclusion of which she offered the following resolutions:

Inasmuch as the Family is the central and supreme institution among human societies, so that all other organizations, whether in Church or State, depend upon it for their character and action, its evils being the source of all evil, and its good the fountain of all good, involved in the destiny of the race; and inasmuch as marriage, the bond of this primary and principal of human association, was the only institution given by the Creator in the innocence of Eden, and is the chosen symbol of relation for the union of the Church to her Redeemer in the

Paradise to come, we are thereby taught as much as we can yet comprehend of the deep significance of its idea and the boundless beneficence of its office.

Resolved, Therefore, that the correction of its abuses is the starting point of all the reforms which the world needs, and that Woman by every fact of her natural constitution, and every circumstance of her actual position, is the fitting minister of its redeeming agency, and that answering to the duties of her great mission, and acting within her appropriate sphere, she is authorized to demand the emancipation of her sex from all the slaveries of law and custom, which hitherto have made and kept her incapable of her heaven-appointed office. And that Woman may perform her duties and fulfill her destiny we demand for her, moral, social, pecuniary and political freedom. We demand that her proper individuality be held sacred, her rational independence respected; her faculties all educated, within their aims and objects freely opened to her aspirations; her physical and mental health justly regarded, and all her natural strength elicited, without limit or restraint, reward or punishment other than the laws of her own nature and of general harmony impose, in order that, with enlightened conscience and untrammeled energies, she may do her proper work and contribute the peculiar elements of the new era of civilization, now opening upon the world, in which love shall overrule force, and equal liberty and justice shall replace the degradation of castes and the oppression of individuals.

Miss ANTHONY offered the following resolutions from Mrs. E. C. STANTON, of Seneca Falls:

Resolved, That it is the duty of the women of those States, in which woman has now by law a right to the property she inherits, to refuse to pay taxes so long as she is unrepresented in the government.

Resolved, That the highest interests of the race demand that man and woman be educated together. The isolation of the sexes in all the plans of business and pleasure is crippling to the intellect of woman and destructive of the best affections of man.

Resolved, That while we rejoice in the fact that we now

have physicians of both soul and body from our own sex, we still feel the need of woman in the legal profession, whose intellect, sharpened by her own interests, may suggest more liberal interpretations of our present laws, or show the necessity of a new code, far better and higher, more wise and just, than that which now disgraces our statute books.

Resolved, That justice requires that the property of woman should not be taxed throughout this state to build and endow the People's College, now proposed, unless woman be fully admitted to share equally with man in all its rights and privileges.

Resolved, We rejoice in the recent temperance movement of the women of this State, and also the treatment their delegates received from our clerical brethren, at the late annual meeting of the State society. A few such encounters will open the eyes of woman to the true character of the Priests and Levites of our day.

Resolved, That our present laws on marriage should be so remodelled that the wife and children of the beastly drunkard and gross libertine may more easily escape from such degrading associations.

LUCY STONE:—I cannot help expressing my gratitude to this Convention for the respectful attention you have given to us this three days' Session. If there has been anything said that has impressed your heart for good, take it to your heart of hearts and act upon it for good. To these women I want to say. Have some object in life worth living for, learn self-help, learn to do good and improve. I remember the words of Miss EMMA EMSBURY—she says, persons may ridicule what they cannot help. Be above all sneers, be calm, be patient and smile on in the sublime height, and the low scoff will all pass away. Every ear that listens to me feels that there are hours coming over us when we feel the need of something more elevating to the soul—when we feel that we need a more perfect character— when we feel as though we were fragments of a being. Again I say, learn self-help and independence. Friends, it will cost us sacrifice—the woman who goes from her sphere will be derided—yet we shall not be alone. As Frederick Douglass said at the Pittsburgh Convention, one with God is a majority.

Her closing speech was most impressive, and, although the hour was late, was listened to with the most profound attention.

Cleveland, Ohio, 1853

William Lloyd Garrison's Address

William Lloyd Garrison, editor of the radical abolition-
ist newspaper, The Liberator, *and a founder of the*
American Anti-Slavery Society in 1833, was also a
strong advocate of women's rights, welcoming women
to full participation in the activities of the Anti-Slavery
Society. An ardent anticlericalist who condemned the
American clergy for its silence on slavery, he could not
resist attacking the clergy for conservatism on the issue
of women's rights. In this speech he accuses the clergy
of hypocrisy for maintaining the sanctity of marriage
while sanctioning the status of "three and a half mil-
lion people" (slaves) who could not marry legally. Gar-
rison, unlike some of the other women's rights advo-
cates, accuses men of being the oppressors of women,
just as slaveholders are the oppressors of slaves.

WILLIAM LLOYD GARRISON said: I have but a few words to
submit to the meeting at the present time. In regard to the
position of the Church and clergy, on the subject of purity, I
think it is sufficient to remind the people here, that whatever
may be the external form observed by the Church toward its
members, pertaining to licentiousness, one thing is noticeable,
and that is, that the marriage relation is abolished among
three and a half millions of people; and the abolition of mar-

Source: Elizabeth Cady Stanton, Susan B. Anthony et al., *The History of*
Woman Suffrage (6 vols.; New York, 1881–1922; reprint, New York, 1969),
vol. 1.

William Lloyd Garrison, editor of *The Liberator. (Courtesy: Boston Public Library Photographic Collection)*

riage on that frightful scale, is in the main sanctioned and sustained by the American Church and clergy. And if this does not involve them in all that is impure, and licentious, and demoralizing, I know not what can do so.

As it respects the objection to our adopting the Declaration of Independence as put forth at Seneca Falls, on the ground that it is a parody, and that, being a parody, it will only excite the mirthfulness of those who hear or read it in that form; I would simply remark, that I very much doubt, whether, among candid and serious men, there would be any such mirthfulness excited. At the time that document was published, I read it, but I had forgotten it till this morning, and on listening to it, my mind was deeply impressed with its pertinacity and its power. It seemed to me, the *argumentum ad hominum*, to this nation. It was measuring the people of this country by their own standard. It was taking their own words and applying their own principles to women, as they have been applied to men. At the same time, I liked the suggestion that we had better present an original paper to the country; and on conferring with the Committee after the adjournment, they agreed that it would be better to have such a paper; and that paper will undoubtedly be prepared, although we are not now ready to lay it before the Convention.

It was this morning objected to the Declaration of Sentiments, that it implied that man was the only transgressor, that he had been guilty of injustice and usurpation, and the suggestion was also made, that woman should not be criminated, in this only, but regarded rather as one who had erred through ignorance; and our eloquent friend, Mrs. Rose, who stood on this platform and pleaded with such marked ability, as she always does plead in any cause she undertakes to speak upon, told us her creed. She told us she did not blame anybody, really, and did not hold any man to be criminal, or any individual to be responsible for public sentiment, as regards the difference of criminality of man and woman.

For my own part, I am not prepared to respect that philosophy. I believe in sin, therefore in a sinner; in theft, therefore in a thief; in slavery, therefore in a slaveholder; in wrong, therefore in a wrong-doer; and unless the men of this nation are made by woman to see that they have been guilty of usurpation, and cruel usurpation, I believe very little progress will be made. To say all this has been done without thinking, without calculation, without design, by mere accident, by a want of light; can anybody believe this who is familiar with all the facts in the case? Certainly, for one, I hope ever to lean to the charitable side, and will try to do so. I, too, believe things are done through misconception and misapprehension, which are injurious, yes, which are immoral and unchristian; but only to a limited extent. There is such a thing as intelligent wickedness, a design on the part of those who have the light to quench it, and to do the wrong to gratify their own propensities, and to further their own interests. So, then, I believe, that as man has monopolized for generations all the rights which belong to woman, it has not been accidental, not through ignorance on his part; but I believe that man has done this through calculation, actuated by a spirit of pride, a desire for domination which has made him degrade woman in her own eyes, and thereby tend to make her a mere vassal.

It seems to me, therefore, that we are to deal with the consciences of men. It is idle to say that the guilt is common, that the women are as deeply involved in this matter as the men. Never can it be said that the victims are as much to be blamed as the victimizer; that the slaves are to be as much blamed as the slaveholders and slave-drivers; that the women who have no rights, are to be as much blamed as the men who have played the part of robbers and tyrants. We must deal with conscience. The men of this nation, and the men of all nations, have no just respect for woman. They have tyrannized over her deliberately, they have not sinned through ignorance, but theirs is not the knowledge that saves. Who can say truly, that in all things he acts up to the light he enjoys, that he does not do something which he knows is not the very thing, or the best thing he ought to do? How few there are among mankind who are able to say this with regard to themselves. Is not the light all around us? Does not this nation know how great its guilt is in enslaving one-sixth of its people? Do not the men of this nation know ever since the landing of the pilgrims, that they are wrong in making subject one-half of the people? Rely upon it, it has not been a mistake on their part. It has been sin. It has been guilt; and they manifest their guilt to a demonstration, in the manner in which they receive this movement. Those who do wrong ignorantly, do not willingly continue in it, when they find they are in the wrong. Ignorance is not an evidence of guilt certainly. It is only an evidence of a want of light. They who are only ignorant, will never rage, and rave, and threaten, and foam, when the light comes; but being interested and walking in the light, will always present a manly front, and be willing to be taught, and be willing to be told they are in the wrong.

Take the case of slavery: How has the anti-slavery cause been received? Not argumentatively, not by reason, not by entering the free arena of fair discussion and comparing notes; the arguments have been rotten eggs, and brickbats and calumny, and in the southern portion of the country, a spirit of murder, and threats to cut out the tongues of those who spoke against them. What has this indicated on the part of the nation? What but conscious guilt? Not ignorance, not that they had not the light. They had the light and rejected it.

How has this Woman's Rights movement been treated in this country, on the right hand and on the left? This nation ridicules and derides this movement, and spits upon it, as fit only to be cast out and trampled underfoot. This is not ignorance. They know all about the truth. It is the natural outbreak of tyranny. It is because the tyrants and usurpers are alarmed. They have been and are called to judgment, and they dread the examination and exposure of their position and character.

Women of America! you have something to blame yourselves for in this matter, something to account for to God and the world. Granted. But then you are the victims in this land, as the women of all lands are, to the tyrannical power and godless ambition of man; and we must show who are responsible in this matter. We must test everybody here. Every one of us must give an account of himself to God. It is an individual testing of character. Mark the man or the woman who derides this movement, who turns his or her back upon it; who is disposed to let misrule keep on, and you will find you have a sure indication of character. You will find that such persons are destitute of principles; for if you can convict a man of being wanting in principle anywhere, it will be everywhere. He who loves the right for its own sake, loves the right everywhere. He who is a man of principle, is a man of principle always. Let me see the man who is willing to have any one of God's rational creatures sacrificed to promote anything, aside from the well-being of that creature himself, and I will show you an unprincipled man.

It is so in this movement. Nobody argues against it, nobody pretends to have an argument. Your platform is free everywhere, wherever these Conventions are held. Yet no man comes forward in a decent, respectable manner, to show you that you are wrong in the charges you bring against the law-makers of the land. There is no argument against it. The thing is self-evident. I should not know how to begin to frame an argument. That which is self-evident is greater than argument, and beyond logic. It testifies of itself. You and I, as human beings, claim to have rights, but I never think of going into an argument with anybody, to prove that I ought to have rights. I have the argument and logic here, it is in my own breast and consciousness; and the logic of the schools becomes contemptible beside these. The more you try to argue, the worse you are off. It is not the place for metaphysics, it is the place for affirmation. Woman is the counterpart of man; she has the same divine image, having the same natural and inalienable rights as man. To state the proposition is enough; it contains the argument, and nobody can gainsay it, in an honorable way.

I rose simply to say, that though I should deprecate making our platform a theological arena, yet believing that men are guilty of intentional wrong, in keeping woman subject, I believe in having them criminated. You talk of injustice, then there is an unjust man somewhere. Even Mrs. Rose could talk of the guilt of society. Society! I know nothing of society. I know the guilt of individuals. Society is an abstract term: it is made up of individuals, and the responsibility rests with individuals. So then, if we are to call men to repentance, there is such a thing as wrong-doing intelligently, sinning against God and man, with light enough to convict us, and to condemn us before God and the world. Let this cause then be pressed upon the hearts and consciences, against those who hold unjust rights in their possession.

"Address to the Legislature
of New York"

Elizabeth Cady Stanton

Elizabeth Cady Stanton's address to the New York legislature on February 14, 1854, was a ringing challenge to the lawmakers. In the six years and countless women's rights meetings since Seneca Falls she had lost her reticence about speaking in public. In this address she drew on her legal knowledge as the daughter of a judge and the wife of a journalist-turned-lawyer to point out the injustices to women under the present legal system. She described in vivid detail how women suffered (1) as women, (2) as wives, (3) as widows, and (4) as mothers. Her speech shocked Judge Cady so much that for a time he threatened to disown his daughter.

TO THE LEGISLATURE OF THE
STATE OF NEW YORK:

"The thinking minds of all nations call for change. There is a deep-lying struggle in the whole fabric of society; a boundless, grinding collision of the New with the Old."

The tyrant, Custom, has been summoned before the bar of Common Sense. His Majesty no longer awes the multitude—his sceptre is broken—his crown is trampled in the dust—the sentence of death is pronounced upon him. All nations, ranks and classes have, in turn, questioned and repudiated his authority; and now, that the monster is chained and caged,

Source: Elizabeth Cady Stanton, "Address to the Legislature of New York," *The Lily* 6, no. 6 (15 Mar. 1854).

Elizabeth Cady Stanton House. This nineteenth-century home where Elizabeth Cady Stanton resided while reflecting on women's rights is preserved in Seneca Falls, N.Y. *(Illustration, courtesy: Women's Rights National Historical Park, Seneca Falls, N.Y.)*

timid woman, on tiptoe, comes to look him in the face, and to demand of her brave sires and sons, who struck stout blows for liberty, if, in this change of dynasty, she, too, shall find relief.

Yes, gentlemen, in republican America, in the 19th century, we, the daughters of the revolutionary heroes of '76, demand at your hands the redress of our grievances—a revision of your State Constitution—a new code of laws. Permit us then, as briefly as possible, to call your attention to the legal disabilities under which we labor.

1st. Look at the position of woman as woman. It is not enough for us that by your laws we are permitted to live and breathe, to claim the necessaries of life from our legal protectors—to pay the penalty of our crimes; we demand the full recognition of all our rights as citizens of the Empire State. We are persons; native, free-born citizens; property-holders, taxpayers; yet we are denied the exercise of our right to the elective franchise.

We support ourselves, and, in part, your schools, colleges, churches, your poor-houses, jails, prisons, the army, the navy, the whole machinery of government, and yet we have no voice in your councils. We have every qualification required by the constitution, necessary to the legal voter, but the one of sex. We are moral, virtuous and intelligent, and in all respects quite equal to the proud white man himself, and yet by your laws we are classed with idiots, lunatics and negroes; and though we do not feel honored by the place assigned us, yet, in fact, our legal position is lower than that of either; for the negro can be raised to the dignity of a voter if he possesses himself of $250; the lunatic can vote in his moments of sanity, and the idiot, too, if he be a male one, and not more than nine-tenths a fool; but we, who have guided great movements of charity, established missions, edited journals, published works on history, economy and statistics; who have governed nations, led armies, filled the professor's chair, taught philosophy and mathematics to the *savants* of our age, discovered planets, piloted ships across the sea, are denied the most sacred rights of citizens, because, forsooth, we came not into this republic crowned with the dignity of manhood! Woman is theoretically absolved from all allegiance to the laws of the State. Sec. 1, Bill of Rights, 2 R.S., 301, says that no authority can, on any pretence whatever, be exercised over the citizens of this State but such as is, or shall be derived from, and *granted by, the people of this State.*

Now, gentlemen, we would fain know by what authority you have disfranchised one-half the people of this State? You who have so boldly taken possession of the bulwarks of this republic, show us your credentials, and thus prove your exclusive right to govern, not only yourselves, but us. Judge Hurlburt, who has long occupied a high place at the bar in this State, and who recently retired with honor from the bench of the supreme court, in his profound work on human rights, has pronounced your present position rank usurpation. Can it be that here, where are acknowledged no royal blood, no apostolic descent, that you, who have declared that all men were created equal—that governments derive their just powers from the consent of the governed, would willingly build up an aristocracy that places the ignorant and vulgar above the educated and refined—the alien and the ditch-digger above the authors and poets of the day—an aristocracy that would raise the sons above the mothers that bore them? Would that the men who can sanction a constitution so opposed to the genius of this government, who can enact and execute laws so degrading to womankind, had sprung, Minerva-like, from the brains of their fathers, that the matrons of this republic need not blush to own their sons! Woman's position, under our free institutions, is much lower than under the monarchy of England. "In England the idea of woman holding official station is not so strange as in the United States. The Countess of Pembroke, Dorset and Montgomery held the office of hereditary sheriff of Westmoreland, and exercised it in person. At the assizes at Appleby, she sat with the judges on the bench. In a reported case, it is stated by counsel, and substantially assented to by the court, that a woman is capable of serving in almost all the offices of the kingdom, such as those of queen, marshal, great chamberlain and constable of England, the champion of England, commissioner of sewers, governor of work house, sexton, keeper of the prison, of the gate house of the dean and chapter of Westminster, returning officer for members of parliament, and constable, the latter of which is in some respects judicial. The office of jailor is frequently exercised by a woman. In the United States a woman may administer on the effects of her deceased husband, and she has occasionally held a subordinate place in the post office department. She has therefore a sort of post mortem, post mistress notoriety; but with the exception of handling letters of administration and letters mailed, she is the submissive creature of the old common law." True, the unmarried woman has a right to the property she inherits and the money she earns, but she is taxed without representation. And here again you place the negro, so unjustly degraded by you, in a superior position to your own wives and mothers; for colored males possessed of a certain amount of property, and certain other qualifications can vote, but if they do not have these qualifications *they are not subject to direct taxation;* wherein they have the advantage of woman, she being subject to taxation for whatever amount she may possess. (Constitution of N.Y., article 2, sec. 2.) But, say you, are not all women sufficiently represented by their fathers, husbands and brothers? Let your statute books answer the question.

Again we demand, in criminal cases, that most sacred of all rights, trial by a jury of our own peers. The establishment of trial by a jury is of so early a date that its beginning is lost in antiquity; but the right of trial by a jury of one's own peers is a great, progressive step of advanced civilization. No rank of men have ever been satisfied with being tried by jurors higher or lower in the civil or political scale than themselves; for jealousy on the one hand, and contempt on the other, has ever effectually blinded the eyes of justice. Hence, all along the pages of history, we find the king, the noble, the peasant, the cardinal, the priest, the layman, each in turn protesting against the authority of the tribunal before which they were summoned to appear. Charles the First refused to recognize the competency of the tribunal which condemned him: For how, said he, can subjects judge a king? The stern descendants of our Pilgrim fathers refused to answer for their crimes before an English Parliament. For how, said they, can a king judge rebels? And shall woman here consent to be tried by the liege lord, who has dubbed himself law-maker, judge, juror, and sheriff, too?—whose power, though sanctioned by Church and State, has no foundation in justice and equity, and is a bold assumption of our inalienable rights. In England a parliament-lord could challenge a jury where a knight was not empanelled. An alien could demand a jury composed half of his own countrymen; or, in some special cases, juries were even constituted entirely of women. Having seen that man fails to do justice to woman in her best estate, to the virtuous, the noble, the true of our sex, should we trust to his tender mercies, the weak, the ignorant, the morally insane? It is not to be denied that the interests of man and woman in the present undeveloped state of the race, and under the existing social arrangements, are and must be antagonistic. The nobleman cannot make just laws for the peasant; the slaveholder for the slave; neither can man make and execute just laws for woman, because in each case, the one in power fails to apply the immutable principles of right to any grade but his own. Shall an erring woman be dragged before a bar of grim-visaged judges, lawyers and jurors, there to be grossly questioned in public on subjects which women scarce breathe in secret to one another? Shall the most sacred relations of life be called up and rudely scanned by men who, by their own admission, are so coarse that women could not meet them even at the polls without contamination? and yet shall she find there no woman's face or voice to pity and defend? Shall the frenzied mother who, to save herself and child from exposure and disgrace, ended the life that had but just begun, be dragged before such a tribunal to answer for her crime? How can man enter into the feelings of that mother? How can he judge of the mighty agonies of soul that impelled her to such an outrage of maternal instincts? How can he weigh the mountain of sorrow that crushed that mother's heart when she wildly tossed her helpless babe into the cold waters of the mighty sea? Where is he who by false vows thus blasted this trusting woman? Had that helpless child no claims on his protection? Ah, he is freely abroad in the dignity of manhood, in the pulpit, in the bench, in the professor's chair. The imprisonment of his victim and the death of his child, detract not a tithe from his standing and complacency. His peers made the law, and shall law-makers lay nets for those of their own rank? Shall laws which come from the logical brain of man take cognizance of violence done to the moral and affectional nature which predominates, as is said, in woman? Statesmen of New York, whose daughters, guarded by your affection, and lapped amidst luxuries which your indulgence spreads, care more for their nodding plumes and velvet trains than for the statute laws by which their persons and properties are held—who, blinded by custom and prejudice to the degraded position which they and their sisters occupy in the civil scale, haughtily claim that they already have all the rights they want, how, think ye, you would feel to see a daughter summoned for such a crime—and remember these daughters are but human—before such a tribunal? Would it not, in that hour, be some consolation to see that she was surrounded by the wise and virtuous of her own sex; by those who had known the depth of a mother's love and the misery of a lover's falsehood; to know that to these she could make her confession, and from them receive her sentence? If so, then listen to our just demands, and make such a change in your laws as will secure to every woman tried in your courts an impartial jury. At this moment among the hundreds of women who are shut up in prisons in this State, not one has enjoyed that most sacred of all rights—that right which you would die to defend for yourselves—trial by a jury of one's peers.

2d. Look at the position of woman as wife.—Your laws relating to marriage—founded as they are on the old common law of England, a compound of barbarous usages, but partially modified by progressive civilization—are in open violation of our enlightened ideas of justice, and of the holiest feelings of our nature. If you take the highest view of marriage, as a Divine relation, which love alone can constitute and sanctify, then of course human legislation can only recognize it.—Man can neither bind or loose its ties, for that prerogative belongs to God alone, who makes man and woman, and the laws of attraction by which they are united. But if you regard marriage as a civil contract, then let it be subject to the same laws which control all other contracts. Do not make it a kind of half-human, half-divine institution which you may build up but cannot regulate. Do not, by your special legislation for this one kind of contract, involve yourselves in the grossest absurdities and contradictions.

So long as by your laws no man can make a contract for a horse or piece of land until he is twenty-one years of age, and by which contract he is not bound if any deception has been practiced, or if the party contracting has not fulfilled his part of the agreement—so long as the parties in all mere civil contracts retain their identity and all the power and independence they had before contracting, with the full right to dissolve all partnerships and contracts for any reason, at the will and option of the parties themselves, upon what principle of civil jurisprudence do you permit the boy of fourteen and the girl of twelve, in violation of every natural law, to make a contract more momentous in importance than any other, and then hold them to it, come what may, the whole of their natural lives, in spite of disappointment, deception and misery? Then, too, the signing of this contract is instant civil death to one of the parties. The woman who but yesterday was sued on bended knee, who stood so high in the scale of being as to make an agreement on equal terms with a proud Saxon man, to-day has no civil existence, no social freedom. The wife who inherits no property holds about the same legal position that does the slave on the southern plantation. She can own nothing, sell nothing. She has no right even to the wages she earns; her person, her time, her services are the property of another. She cannot testify in many cases, against her husband. She can get no redress for her wrongs in her own name in any court of justice. She can neither sue nor be sued. She is not held morally responsible for any crime committed in the presence of her husband, so completely is her very existence supposed by the law to be merged in that of another. Think of it; your wives may be thieves, libellers, burglars, incendiaries, and for crimes like these they are not held amenable to the laws of the land, if they but commit them in your dread presence.—For them, alas! there is no higher law than the will of man. Herein behold the bloated conceit of these Petruchios of the law, who seem to say:

> "Nay, look not big, nor stamp, nor stare, nor fret,
> I will be master of what is mine own;
> She is my goods, my chattels; she is my house,
> My household stuff, my field, my barn,
> My horse, my ox, my ass, my anything;
> And here she stands, touch her whoever dare..."

How could man ever look thus on woman?—She, at whose feet Socrates learned wisdom—she, who gave to the world a Saviour, and witnessed alike the adoration of the Magi and the agonies of the cross. How could such a being, so blessed and honored, ever become the ignoble, servile, cringing slave, with whom the fear of man could be paramount to the sacred dictates of conscience and the holy love of Heaven? By the common law of England, the spirit of which has been but too faithfully incorporated into our statute law, a husband has a right to whip his wife with a rod not larger than his thumb, to shut her up in a room, and administer whatever moderate chastisement he may deem necessary to insure obedience to his wishes, and for her healthful moral development! He can forbid all persons harboring or trusting her on his account. He can deprive her of all social intercourse with her nearest and dearest friends. If by great economy she accumulates a small sum, which for future need she deposit, little by little, in a Savings Bank, the husband has a right to draw it out, at his option, to use it as he may see fit.

"Husband is entitled to wife's credit or business talents (whenever their intermarriage may have occurred;) and goods purchased by her on her own credit, with his consent, while cohabiting with him, can be seized and sold in execution against him for his own debts, and this, though she carry on business in her own name."—7 *Howard's Practice. Report, 105, Lovett agt. Robinson and Witbeck, sheriff, &c.*

"No letters of administration shall be granted to a person convicted of infamous crime; nor to any one incapable by law of making a contract; nor to a person not a citizen of the United States, unless such person reside within this State; nor to any one who is under twenty-one years of age; nor to any peron who shall be judged incompetent by the surrogate to execute duties of such trust, by reason of drunkenness, improvidence, or want of understanding, nor any married woman; but where a married woman is entitled to administration, the same may be granted to her husband in her right and behalf."

There is nothing that an unruly wife might do against which the husband has not sufficient protection in the law. But not so with the wife. If she have a worthless husband, a confirmed drunkard, a villain or a vagrant, he has still all the rights of a man, a husband and a father. Though the whole support of the family be thrown upon the wife, if the wages she earns be paid to her by her employer, the husband can receive them again.—If, by unwearied industry and perseverance, she can earn for herself and children a patch of ground and a shed to cover them, the husband can strip her of all her hard earnings, turn her and her little ones out in the cold northern blast, take the clothes from their backs, the bread from their mouths; all this by your laws he may do, and he has done, oft and again, to satisfy the rapacity of that monster in human form, the rumseller.

But the wife who is so fortunate as to have inherited property, has, by the new law in this State, been redeemed from her lost condition. She is no longer a legal nonentity. This property law, if fairly construed, will overturn the whole code relating to woman and property. The right to property implies the right to buy and sell, to will and bequeath, and herein is the dawning of a civil existence for woman, for now the "femme covert" must have the right to make contracts. So, get ready, gentlemen; the "little justice" will be coming to you one day, deed in hand, for your acknowledgment. When he asks you "if you sign without fear or compulsion," say yes, boldly, as we do. Then, too, the right to will is ours. Now what becomes of the "tenant for life?" Shall he, the happy husband of a millionaire, who has lived in yonder princely mansion in the midst of plenty and elegance, be cut down in a day to the use of one-third of this estate and a few hundred a year, as long as he remains her widower? And should he, in spite of his bounty on celibacy, impelled by his affections, marry again, choosing for a wife a woman as poor as himself, shall he be thrown penniless on the cold world—this child of fortune enervated by ease and luxury, henceforth to be dependent wholly on his own resources? Poor man! He would be rich, though, in the *sympathies* of many women who have passed through just such an ordeal. But what is property without the right to protect that property by law? It is mockery to say a certain estate is mine, if, without my consent, you have the right to tax me when and how you please, while I have no voice in making the tax-gatherer, the legislator or the law. The right to property will, of necessity, compel us in due time to the exercise of our right to the elective franchise, and then naturally follows the right to hold office.

3d. Look at the position of woman as widow. Whenever we attempt to point out the wrongs of the wife, those who would have us believe that the laws cannot be improved, point us to the privileges, powers and claims of the widow. Let us look into these a little. Behold in yonder humble house a married pair, who, for long years, have lived together, childless and alone. These few acres of well tilled land, with the small white house that looks so cheerful through its vines and flowers, attest the honest thrift and simple taste of its owners. This man and woman, by their hard days' labor, have made this home their own. Here they live in peace and plenty, happy in the hope that they may dwell together securely under their own vine and figtree for the few years that remain to them, and that under the shadow of these trees, planted by their own hands, and in the midst of their household goods, so loved and familiar, here may take their farewell of earth. But, alas for human hopes! the husband dies, and without will, and the stricken widow, at one fell blow, loses the companion of her youth, her house and home, and half the little sum she had in bank. For the law, which takes no cognizance of widows left with twelve children and not one cent, instantly spies out this widow, takes account of her effects, and announces to her the startling intelligence that but one-third of the house and lot, and one half the personal property, are hers. The law has other favorites with whom she must share the hard-earned savings of years. In this dark hour of grief, the coarse minions of the law gather round the widow's hearth-stone, and in the name of justice, outrage all natural sense of right; mock at the sacredness of human love, and with cold familiarity proceed to place a monied value on the old arm chair, in which, but a few brief hours since, she closed the eyes that had ever beamed on her with kindness and affection; on the solemn clock in the corner, that told the hour he passed away; on every garment with which his form and presence were associated, and on every article of comfort and convenience that the house contained, even down to the knives and forks and spoons—and the widow saw it all—and when the work was done, she gathered up what the law allowed her and went forth to seek her another home! This is the much talked of widow's dower. Behold the magnanimity of the law in allowing the widow to retain a life interest in one-third the landed estate, and one-half the personal property of her husband, and taking the lion's share to itself! Had she died first, the house and land would all have been her husband's still. No one would have dared to intrude upon the privacy of his home, or to molest him in his sacred retreat of sorrow.

How, I ask you, can that be called justice, which makes such a distinction as this between man and woman?

By management, economy and industry, our widow is able, in a few years, to redeem her house and home. But the law never loses sight of the purse, no matter how low in the scale of being its owner may be. It sends its officers round every year to gather in the harvest for the public crib, and no widow who owns a piece of land two feet square ever escapes this reckoning. Our widow, too, who has now twice earned her home, has her annual tax to pay also—a tribute of gratitude that she is permitted to breathe the free air of this republic, where "taxation without representation," by such worthies as John Hancock and Samuel Adams, has been declared "intolerable tyranny." Having glanced at the magnanimity of the law in its dealings with the widow, let us see how the individual man, under the influence of such laws, doles out justice to his helpmate. The husband has the absolute right to will away his property as he may see fit. If he has children, he can divide his property among them, leaving his wife her third only of the landed estate, thus making her a dependent on the bounty of her children. A man with thirty thousand dollars in personal property, may leave his wife but a few hundred a year, as long as she remains his widow.

The cases are without number where women, who have lived in ease and elegance, at the death of their husbands have, by will, been reduced to the bare necessaries of life. The man who leaves his wife the sole guardian of his property and children is an exception to the general rule. Man has ever manifested a wish that the world should indeed be a blank to the companion whom he leaves behind him. The Hindoo makes that wish a law, and burns the widow on the funeral pile of her husband; but the civilized man, impressed with a different view of the sacredness of life, takes a less summary mode of drawing his beloved partner after him; he does it by the deprivation and starvation of the flesh, and the humiliation and mortification of the spirit. In bequeathing to the wife just enough to keep soul and body together, man seems to lose sight of the fact that woman, like himself, takes great pleasure in acts of benevolence and charity. It is but just, therefore, that she should have it in her power to give during her life, and to will away at her death, as her benevolence or obligations might prompt her to do.

4th. Look at the position of woman as *mother*. There is no human love so generous, strong and steadfast as that of the mother for her child; yet behold how cruel and ruthless are your laws touching this most sacred relation.

Nature has clearly made the mother the guardian of the child; but man, in his inordinate love of power, does continually set nature and nature's laws at open defiance. The father may apprentice his child, bind him out to a trade or labor, without the mother's consent—yea, in direct opposition to her most earnest entreaties, her prayers and tears.

He may apprentice his son to a gamester or rumseller, and thus cancel his debts of *honor*. By the abuse of this absolute power, he may bind his daughter to the owner of a brothel, and, by the degradation of his child, supply his daily wants; and such things, gentlemen, have been done in our very midst. Moreover, the father, about to die, may bind out all his children wherever and to whomsoever he may see fit, and thus, in fact, will away the guardianship of all his children from the mother. The Revised Statutes of New York provide that "every father, whether of full age or a minor, of a child to be born, or of any living child under the age of twenty-one years, and unmarried, may by his *deed or last will*, duly executed, dispose of the custody and tuition of such child during its minority, or for any less time, to any person or persons, in possession or remainder." 2 R.S., page 150, sec. 1.

Thus, by your laws, the child is the absolute property of the father, wholly at his disposal in life or at death.

In case of separation, the law gives the children to the father; no matter what his character or condition. At this very time we can point you to noble, virtuous, well educated mothers in this State, who have abandoned their husbands for their profligacy and confirmed drunkenness. All these have been robbed of their children, who are in the custody of the husband, under the care of his relatives, whilst the mothers are permitted to see them but at stated intervals. But, said one of these mothers, with a grandeur of attitude and manner worthy the noble Roman matron in the palmiest days of that republic, I would rather never see my child again, than be the medium to hand down the low, animal nature of its father, to stamp degradation on the brow of another innocent being. It is enough that one child of his shall call me mother. If you are far sighted statesmen, and do wisely judge of the interests of this commonwealth, you will so shape your future laws as to encourage woman to take the high moral ground that the father of her children must be great and good.

Instead of your present laws, which make the mother and her children the victims of vice and license, you might rather pass laws prohibiting to all drunkards, libertines and fools, the rights of husbands and fathers. Do not the hundreds of laughing idiots that are crowding into our asylums, appeal to the wisdom of our statesmen for some new laws on marriage—to the mothers of this day for a higher, purer morality?

Again, as the condition of the child always follows that of the mother, and as by the abuse of your laws the father may beat the mother, so may he the child. What mother cannot bear me witness to untold sufferings which cruel, vindictive fathers have visited upon their helpless children? Who ever saw a human being that would not abuse unlimited power? Base and ignoble must that man be, who, let the provocation be what it may, would strike a woman; but he who would lacerate a trembling child is unworthy the name of man. A mother's love can be no protection to a child; she cannot appeal to you to save it from a father's cruelty, for the laws take no cognizance of the mother's most grievous wrongs. Neither at home nor abroad can a mother protect her son. Look at the temptations that surround the paths of our youth at every step; look at the gambling and drinking saloons, the club rooms, the dens of infamy and abomination that infest all our villages and cities—slowly but surely sapping the very foundations of all virtue and strength.

By your laws, all these abominable resorts are permitted. It is folly to talk of a mother's moulding the character of her son, when all mankind, backed up by law and public sentiment, conspire to destroy her influence. But when woman's moral power shall speak through the ballot box, then shall her influence be seen and felt; then, in our legislative debates, such questions as the canal tolls on salt, the improvement of rivers and harbors, and the claims of Mr. Smith for damages against the State, would be secondary to the consideration of the legal existence of all these public resorts, which lure our youth on to excessive indulgence and destruction.

Many times and oft it has been asked us, with unaffected seriousness, "what do you women want? What are you aiming at?" Many have manifested a laudable curiosity to know what the wives and daughters could complain of in republican America, where their sires and sons have so bravely fought for freedom and gloriously secured their independence, trampling all tyranny, bigotry and caste in the dust, and declaring to a waiting world the divine truth that all men are created equal.—What can *woman* want under such a government? Admit a radical difference in sex and you demand different spheres—water for fish and air for birds.

It is impossible to make the southern planter believe that his slave feels and reasons just as he does—that injustice and subjection are as galling as to him—that the degradation of living by the will of another, the mere dependent on his caprice, at the mercy of his passions, is as keenly felt by him as his master. If you can force on his unwilling vision a vivid picture of the negro's wrongs, and for a moment touch his soul, his logic brings him instant consolation. He says, the slave does not feel this as I would. Here, gentlemen, is our difficulty: When we plead our cause before the law makers and *savans* of the republic, they cannot take in the idea that men and women are alike; and so long as the masses rest in this delusion, the public mind will not be so much startled by the revelations made of the injustice and degradation of woman's position as by the fact that she should at length wake up to a sense of it.

If you, too, are thus deluded, what avails it that we show by your statute books that your laws are unjust—that woman is the victim of avarice and power? What avails it if we point out the wrongs of women in social life; the victim of passion and lust? You scorn the thought that she has any natural love of freedom burning in her breast, any clear perception of justice urging her on to demand her rights.

Would to God you could know the burning indignation that fills woman's soul when she turns over the pages of your statute books, and sees there how like feudal barons you freemen hold your women. Would that you could know the humiliation she feels for her sex, when she thinks of all the beardless boys in your law offices, learning these ideas of one-sided justice—taking their first lesson in contempt for all womankind—being indoctrinated into the incapacities of their mothers, and the lordly, absolute rights of man over all women, children and property, and to know that these are to be our future Presidents, Judges, Husbands and Fathers; in sorrow we exclaim, alas! for that nation whose sons bow not in loyalty to woman. The mother is the first object of the child's veneration and love, and they who root out this holy sentiment, dream not of the blighting effect it has on the boy and the man. The impression left on law students, fresh from your statute books, is most unfavorable to woman's influence; hence you see but few lawyers chivalrous and high-toned in their sentiments toward woman. They cannot escape the legal view which, by constant reading, has become familiarized to their minds: *"Femme covert,"* "dower," "widow's claims," "protection," "incapacities," "encumbrance," is written on the brow of every woman they meet.

But if, gentlemen, you take the ground that the sexes are alike, and, therefore, you are our faithful representatives—then why all these special laws for woman? Would not one code answer for all of like needs and wants? Christ's golden rule is better than all the special legislation that the ingenuity of man can devise: "Do unto others as you would have others do unto you." This, men and brethren, is all we ask at your hands. We *ask* no better laws than those you have made for yourselves. We need no other protection than that which your present laws secure to you.

In conclusion, then, let us say, in behalf of the women of this State, we ask for all that you have asked for yourselves in the progress of your development, since the Mayflower cast anchor side Plymouth Rock; and simply on the ground that the rights of every human being are the same and identical.

Cincinnati, Ohio, 1855

The effects of women's rights can be seen in the wedding of Lucy Stone, a feminist who married Henry Blackwell, the brother of Elizabeth Blackwell, the first woman to attain a medical degree. When Lucy and Henry married, they drew up the following document, which they signed and had read as part of their wedding ceremony. The minister, himself an abolitionist and women's rights advocate, sent the document and his approbation of it, to William Lloyd Garrison for publication in The Liberator.

MARRIAGE OF LUCY STONE UNDER PROTEST.

It was my privilege to celebrate May day by officiating at a wedding in a farm-house among the hills of West Brookfield. The bridegroom was a man of tried worth, a leader in the Western Anti-Slavery Movement; and the bride was one whose fair name is known throughout the nation; one whose rare intellectual qualities are excelled by the private beauty of her heart and life.

I never perform the marriage ceremony without a renewed sense of the iniquity of our present system of laws in respect to marriage; a system by which "man and wife are one, and that one is the husband." It was with my hearty concurrence, therefore, that the following protest was read and signed, as a part

Source: Elizabeth Cady Stanton, Susan B. Anthony et al., *The History of Woman Suffrage* (6 vols.; New York, 1881–1922; reprint, New York, 1969), vol. 1.

Lucy Stone. *(Courtesy: Boston Public Library Photographic Collection)*

of the nuptial ceremony; and I send it to you, that others may be induced to do likewise.

REV. THOMAS WENTWORTH HIGGINSON.

PROTEST.

While acknowledging our mutual affection by publicly assuming the relationship of husband and wife, yet in justice to ourselves and a great principle, we deem it a duty to declare that this act on our part implies no sanction of, nor promise of voluntary obedience to such of the present laws of marriage, as refuse to recognize the wife as an independent, rational being, while they confer upon the husband an injurious and unnatural superiority, investing him with legal powers which no honorable man would exercise, and which no man should possess. We protest especially against the laws which give to the husband:

1. The custody of the wife's person.
2. The exclusive control and guardianship of their children.
3. The sole ownership of her personal, and use of her real estate, unless previously settled upon her, or placed in the hands of trustees, as in the case of minors, lunatics, and idiots.
4. The absolute right to the product of her industry.

5. Also against laws which give to the widower so much larger and more permanent an interest in the property of his deceased wife, than they give to the widow in that of the deceased husband.

6. Finally, against the whole system by which "the legal existence of the wife is suspended during marriage," so that in most States, she neither has a legal part in the choice of her residence, nor can she make a will, nor sue or be sued in her own name, nor inherit property.

We believe that personal independence and equal human rights can never be forfeited, except for crime; that marriage should be an equal and permanent partnership, and so recognized by law; that until it is so recognized, married partners should provide against the radical injustice of present laws, by every means in their power.

We believe that where domestic difficulties arise, no appeal should be made to legal tribunals under existing laws, but that all difficulties should be submitted to the equitable adjustment of arbitrators mutually chosen.

Thus reverencing law, we enter our protest against rules and customs which are unworthy of the name, since they violate justice, the essence of law.

(Signed),

HENRY B. BLACKWELL,

LUCY STONE.

*   *   *

Lucy Stone, along with Elizabeth Cady Stanton, Lucretia Mott, Susan B. Anthony, and others, would spend most of her adult life in the cause of women's rights. In this excerpt from her address to a women's convention in Cincinnati in 1855, she argues not only for equal rights for women, but equal pay for equal work. She looks to the day when women will routinely seek careers in business and in the professions, citing some notable examples of women who have dared to venture out of traditional gender roles.

LUCY STONE'S SPEECH, 1855

LUCY STONE said: The last speaker alluded to this movement as being that of a few disappointed women. From the first years to which my memory stretches, I have been a disappointed woman. When, with my brothers, I reached forth after the sources of knowledge, I was reproved with "It isn't fit for you; it doesn't belong to women." Then there was but one college in the world where women were admitted, and that was in Brazil. I would have found my way there, but by the time I was prepared to go, one was opened in the young State of Ohio—the first in the United States where women and negroes could enjoy opportunities with white men. I was disappointed when I came to seek a profession worthy an immortal being—every employment was closed to me, except those of the teacher, the seamstress, and the housekeeper. In education, in marriage, in religion, in everything, disappointment is the lot of woman. It shall be the business of my life to deepen this disappointment in every woman's heart until she bows down to it no longer. I wish that women, instead of being walking show-cases, instead of begging of their fathers and brothers the latest and gayest new bonnet, would ask of them their rights.

The question of Woman's Rights is a practical one. The notion has prevailed that it was only an ephemeral idea; that it was but women claiming the right to smoke cigars in the streets, and to frequent bar-rooms. Others have supposed it a question of comparative intellect; others still, of sphere. Too much has already been said and written about woman's sphere. Trace all the doctrines to their source and they will be found to have no basis except in the usages and prejudices of the age. This is seen in the fact that what is tolerated in woman in one country is not tolerated in another. In this country women may hold prayer-meetings, etc., but in Mohammedan countries it is written upon their mosques, "Women and dogs, and other impure animals, are not permitted to enter." Wendell Phillips says, "The best and greatest thing one is capable of doing, that is his sphere." I have confidence in the Father to believe that when He gives us the capacity to do anything He does not make a blunder. Leave women, then, to find their sphere. And do not tell us before we are born even, that our province is to cook dinners, darn stockings, and sew on buttons. We are told woman has all the rights she wants; and even women, I am ashamed to say, tell us so. They mistake the politeness of men for rights—seats while men stand in this hall to-night, and their adulations; but these are mere courtesies. We want rights. The flour-merchant, the house-builder, and the postman charge us no less on account of our sex; but when we endeavor to earn money to pay all these, then, indeed, we find the difference. Man, if he have energy, may hew out for himself a path where no mortal has ever trod, held back by nothing but what is in himself; the world is all before him, where to choose; and we are glad for you, brothers, men, that it is so. But the same society that drives forth the young man, keeps woman at home—a dependent—working little cats on worsted, and little dogs on punctured paper; but if she goes heartily and bravely to give herself to some worthy purpose, she is out of her sphere and she loses caste. Women working in tailor-shops are paid one-third as much as men. Some one in Philadelphia has stated that women make fine shirts for twelve and a half cents apiece; that no woman can make more than nine a week, and the sum thus earned, after deducting rent, fuel, etc., leaves her just three and a half cents a day for bread. Is it a wonder that women are driven to prostitution? Female teachers in New York are paid fifty dollars a year, and for every such situation there are five hundred applicants. I know not what you believe of God, but I believe He gave yearnings and longings to be filled, and that He did not mean all our time should be devoted to feeding and clothing the body. The present condition of woman causes a horrible perversion of the marriage relation. It is asked of a lady, "Has she married well?" "Oh, yes, her husband is rich." Woman must marry for a home, and you men are the sufferers by this; for a woman who loathes you may marry you because you have the means to get money which she can not have. But when woman can enter the lists with you and make money for herself, she will marry you only for deep and earnest affection.

I am detaining you too long, many of you standing, that I

ought to apologize, but women have been wronged so long that I may wrong you a little. (Applause). A woman undertook in Lowell to sell shoes to ladies. Men laughed at her, but in six years she has run them all out, and has a monopoly of the trade. Sarah Tyndale, whose husband was an importer of china, and died bankrupt, continued his business, paid off his debts, and has made a fortune and built the largest china warehouse in the world. (Mrs. Mott here corrected Lucy. Mrs. Tyndale has not the largest china warehouse, but the largest assortment of china in the world). Mrs. Tyndale, herself, drew the plan of her warehouse, and it is the best plan ever drawn. A laborer to whom the architect showed it, said: "Don't she know e'en as much as some men?" I have seen a woman at manual labor turning out chair-legs in a cabinet-shop, with a dress short enough not to drag in the shavings. I wish other women would imitate her in this. It made her hands harder and broader, it is true, but I think a hand with a dollar and a quarter a day in it, better than one with a crossed ninepence. The men in the shop didn't use tobacco, nor swear—they can't do those things where there are women, and we owe it to our brothers to go wherever they work to keep them decent. The widening of woman's sphere is to improve her lot. Let us do it, and if the world scoff, let it scoff—if it sneer, let it sneer—but we will go on emulating the example of the sisters Grimké and Abby Kelly. When they first lectured against slavery they were not listened to as respectfully as you listen to us. So the first female physician meets many difficulties, but to the next the path will be made easy.

Lucretia Mott has been a preacher for years; her right to do so is not questioned among Friends. But when Antoinette Brown felt that she was commanded to preach, and to arrest the progress of thousands that were on the road to hell; why, when she applied for ordination they acted as though they had rather the whole world should go to hell, than that Antoinette Brown should be allowed to tell them how to keep out of it. She is now ordained over a parish in the State of New York, but when she meets on the Temperance platform the Rev. John Chambers, or your own Gen. Carey (applause) they greet her with hisses. Theodore Parker said: "The acorn that the school-boy carries in his pocket and the squirrel stows in his cheek, has in it the possibility of an oak, able to withstand, for ages, the cold winter and the driving blast." I have seen the acorn men and women, but never the perfect oak; all are but abortions. The young mother, when first the new-born babe nestles in her bosom, and a heretofore unknown love springs up in her heart, finds herself unprepared for this new relation in life, and she sends forth the child scarred and dwarfed by her own weakness and imbecility, as no stream can rise higher than its fountain.

THE HISTORY
AS PARTICIPANTS
REMEMBERED IT

History of Woman Suffrage
(1881–1886)

Elizabeth Cady Stanton and
Susan B. Anthony

*Toward the end of their work in the feminist cause, the
two women who had labored together for so many years
undertook to compile a history of one of the most radical ambitions of the women's movement: woman suffrage. In an impressive and now invaluable work, they
wrote and edited three volumes between 1881 and 1886.
A fourth volume appeared in 1902, the year of Elizabeth
Cady Stanton's death, and the final two volumes, edited
by Ida Husted Harper, Stanton's biographer, were published in 1922. The following is the account of the historic meeting in Seneca Falls.*

On Sunday morning [July 16, 1848] they met in Mrs.
McClintock's parlor to write their declaration, resolutions, and
to consider subjects for speeches. As the convention was to
assemble in three days, the time was short for such productions; but having no experience in the *modus operandi* of getting up conventions, nor in that kind of literature, they were
quite innocent of the herculean labors they proposed. On
the first attempt to frame a resolution; to crowd a complete
thought, clearly and concisely, into three lines; they felt as
helpless and hopeless as if they had been suddenly asked to

Source: Elizabeth Cady Stanton, Susan B. Anthony et al., *The History of
Woman Suffrage* (6 vols.; New York, 1881–1922; reprint, New York, 1969),
vol. 1.

Susan B. Anthony. *(Courtesy: Library of Congress)*

construct a steam engine. And the humiliating fact may as well now be recorded that before taking the initiative step, those ladies resigned themselves to a faithful perusal of various masculine productions. The reports of Peace, Temperance, and Anti-Slavery conventions were examined, but all alike seemed too tame and pacific for the inauguration of a rebellion such as the world had never before seen. They knew women had wrongs, but how to state them was the difficulty, and this was increased from the fact that they themselves were fortunately organized and conditioned; they were neither "sour old maids," "childless women," nor "divorced wives," as the newspapers declared them to be. While they had felt the insults incident to sex, in many ways, as every proud, thinking woman must, in the laws, religion, and literature of the world, and in the invidious and degrading sentiments and customs of all nations, yet they had not in their own experience endured the coarser forms of tyranny resulting from unjust laws, or association with immoral and unscrupulous men, but they had souls large enough to feel the wrongs of others, without being scarified in their own flesh.

After much delay, one of the circle took up the Declaration of 1776, and read it aloud with much spirit and emphasis, and it was at once decided to adopt the historic document, with some slight changes such as substituting "all men" for "King George." Knowing that women must have more to complain of than men under any circumstances possibly could, and seeing the Fathers had eighteen grievances, a protracted search was made through statute books, church usages, and the customs of society to find that exact number. Several well-disposed men assisted in collecting the grievances, until, with the announcement of the eighteenth, the women felt they had enough to go before the world with a good case. One youthful lord remarked, "Your grievances must be grievous indeed, when you are obliged to go to books in order to find them out."

The eventful day dawned at last, and crowds in carriages and on foot, wended their way to the Wesleyan church. When those having charge of the Declaration, the resolutions, and several volumes of the Statutes of New York arrived on the scene, lo! the door was locked. However, an embryo Professor of Yale College was lifted through an open window to unbar the door; that done, the church was quickly filled. It had been decided to have no men present, but as they were already on the spot, and as the women who must take the responsibility of organizing the meeting, and leading the discussions, shrank from doing either, it was decided, in a hasty council round the altar, that this was an occasion when men might make themselves pre-eminently useful. It was agreed they should remain, and take the laboring oar through the Convention.

James Mott, tall and dignified, in Quaker costume, was called to the chair; Mary McClintock appointed Secretary, Frederick Douglass, Samuel Tillman, Ansel Bascom, E. W. Capron, and Thomas McClintock took part throughout in the discussions. Lucretia Mott, accustomed to public speaking in the Society of Friends, stated the objects of the Convention, and in taking a survey of the degraded condition of woman the world over, showed the importance of inaugurating some movement for her education and elevation. Elizabeth and Mary McClintock, and Mrs. Stanton, each read a well-written speech; Martha Wright read some satirical articles she had published in the daily papers answering the diatribes on woman's sphere. Ansel Bascom, who had been a member of the Constitutional

Wesleyan Chapel as partially restored. This site of the first women's rights convention in 1848 was the birthplace of American feminism. An adjacent visitor's center houses exhibits on the history of women's rights. *(Courtesy: Women's Rights National Historical Park, Seneca Falls, N.Y.)*

Convention recently held in Albany, spoke at length on the property bill for married women, just passed the Legislature, and the discussion on woman's rights in that Convention. Samuel Tillman, a young student of law, read a series of the most exasperating statutes for women, from English and American jurists, all reflecting the *tender mercies* of men toward their wives, in taking care of their property and protecting them in their civil rights.

The Declaration having been freely discussed by many present, was re-read by Mrs. Stanton, and with some slight amendments adopted. . . .

At the last session Lucretia Mott offered and spoke to the following resolution:

Resolved, That the speedy success of our cause depends upon the zealous and untiring efforts of both men and women, for the overthrow of the monopoly of the pulpit, and for the securing to woman an equal participation with men in the various trades, professions, and commerce.

The only resolution that was not unanimously adopted was the ninth, urging the women of the country to secure to themselves the elective franchise. Those who took part in the debate feared a demand for the right to vote would defeat others they deemed more rational, and make the whole movement ridiculous.

But Mrs. Stanton and Frederick Douglass seeing that the power to choose rulers and make laws, was the right by which all others could be secured, persistently advocated the resolution, and at last carried it by a small majority.

Thus it will be seen that the Declaration and resolutions in the very first Convention, demanded all the most radical friends of the movement have since claimed—such as equal rights in the universities, in the trades and professions; the right to vote; to share in all political offices, honors, and emoluments; to complete equality in marriage, to personal freedom, property, wages, children; to make contracts; to sue, and be sued; and to testify in courts of justice. At this time the condition of married women under the Common Law, was nearly as degraded as that of the slave on the Southern plantation. The Convention continued through two entire days, and late into the evenings. The deepest interest was manifested to its close.

The proceedings were extensively published, unsparingly ridiculed by the press, and denounced by the pulpit, much to the surprise and chagrin of the leaders. Being deeply in earnest, and believing their demands pre-eminently wise and just, they were wholly unprepared to find themselves the target for the jibes and jeers of the nation. The Declaration was signed by one hundred men, and women, many of whom withdrew their names as soon as the storm of ridicule began to break. The comments of the press were carefully preserved, and it is curious to see that the same old arguments, and objections rife at the start, are reproduced by the press of to-day. But the brave protests sent out from this Convention touched a responsive chord in the hearts of women all over the country.

Conventions were held soon after in Ohio, Massachusetts, Indiana, Pennsylvania, and at different points in New York.

SELECTED READINGS

Andolsen, Barbara H. *"Daughters of Jefferson, Daughters of Boot-blacks": Racism and American Feminism* (Macon, GA: Mercer University Press, 1986).

Bartlett, Elizabeth A. *Liberty, Equality, Sorority: The Origins and Inter-pretation of American Feminist Thought: Frances Wright, Sarah Grimké, and Margaret Fuller* (Brooklyn: Carlson, 1994).

Basch, Norma. *In the Eyes of the Law: Women, Marriage, and Property in Nineteenth-Century New York* (Ithaca: Cornell University Press, 1982).

Berg, Barbara. *The Remembered Gate: Origins of American Feminism* (New York: Oxford University Press, 1978).

Bloomer, Dexter C. *The Life and Writings of Amelia Bloomer* (New York: Schocken Books, 1975).

Chevigny, Bell G. *The Woman and the Myth: Margaret Fuller's Life and Writings* (Old Westbury, NY: Feminist Press, 1976).

Cott, Nancy. *The Bonds of Womanhood: "Woman's Sphere" in New England, 1780–1835* (New Haven: Yale University Press, 1977).

Ellen Carol Dubois, ed. *The Elizabeth Cady Stanton–Susan B. Anthony Reader: Correspondence, Writings, Speeches* (Boston: Northeastern University Press, 1981).

Epstein, Barbara. *The Politics of Domesticity: Women, Evangelism and Temperance in Nineteenth-Century America* (Middletown, CT: Wesleyan University Press, 1981).

Flexner, Eleanor. *Century of Struggle: The Woman's Rights Movement in the United States*, rev. ed. (Cambridge: Belknap Press, 1975).

Foner, Philip S. *Frederick Douglass on Women's Rights* (Westport, CT: Greenwood Press, 1976).

Gilbert, Olive. *Narrative of Sojourner Truth* (New York: Arno Press, 1968).

Gutman, Herbert. *The Black Family in Slavery and Freedom* (New York: Pantheon Books, 1976).

Hallowell, Anna D. *James and Lucretia Mott: Life and Letters* (Boston: Houghton, Mifflin and Co., 1884).

Harper, Ida H. *The Life and Work of Susan B. Anthony* (Indianapolis: Hollenbeck Press, 1908).

Hewitt, Nancy A. *Women's Activism and Social Change: Rochester, New York, 1822–1872* (Ithaca: Cornell University Press, 1984).

Lerner, Gerda. *The Grimké Sisters from South Carolina: Pioneers for Woman's Rights and Abolition* (New York: Schocken, 1966).

Melder, Keith. *Beginnings of Sisterhood: The American Woman's Rights Movement, 1800–1850* (New York: Schocken Books, 1977).

Mills, Bruce. *Culture Reformations: Lydia Maria Child and the Literature of Reform* (Athens, GA: University of Georgia Press, 1994).

Pellauer, Mary D. *Towards a Tradition of Feminist Theology: The Religious Thought of Elizabeth Cady Stanton, Susan B. Anthony, and Anna Howard Shaw* (Brooklyn: Carlson, 1991).

Robinson, Harriet J. H. *Loom and Spindle: or, Life among the Early Mill Girls, with a Sketch of the "Lowell Offering" and some of Its Contributors*, rev. ed. (Kailua, HI: Press Pacifica, 1976).

Solomon, Martha. *A Voice of Their Own: The Woman Suffrage Press, 1840–1910* (Tuscaloosa: University of Alabama Press, 1991).

Stanton, Elizabeth Cady. *Eighty Years and More: Reminiscences, 1815–1897* (New York: T. Fisher Unwin, 1898; reprinted, New York: Schocken Books, 1971).

Welter, Barbara. "The Cult of True Womanhood," *Dimity Convictions: The American Woman in the Nineteenth Century* (Athens: Ohio University Press, 1976).